Crony Capitalism in America

Crony Capitalism in America

2008–2012

Hunter Lewis

|AC²|

AC² Books
94 Landfill Road
Edinburg, VA 22824
888.542.9467   info@AC2Books.com

Publisher's Cataloging-in-Publication Data
(Provided by Quality Books, Inc.)

Lewis, Hunter.
    Crony capitalism in America, 2008-2012 / Hunter Lewis.
    p. cm.
    Includes bibliographical references and index.
    LCCN 2013938294
    ISBN 978-0-9887267-2-7

    1. Capitalism--United States. 2. Financial crisis--United States. 3. Financial institutions--United States--Management. 4. Capitalists and financiers--United States. 5. United States--Economic policy. 6. United States--Economic conditions. I. Title.

HB501.L49 2013
330.12'2

                        QBI13-600070

Contents

Part Nine: Losers

Part Ten: Democracy and Crony Capitalism

Part Eleven: Solutions

Part 1

Introduction

1

Crony Capitalism around the World

ALTHOUGH THIS BOOK is about crony capitalism in America, it is sometimes easier to see more clearly what is not right before our eyes. We will therefore start with a brief tour of crony capitalism abroad, and then decide how much of this applies to us at home. The first stop of our tour will be post-Communist Russia.

In Russia today, failing companies have the usual choice: make changes necessary to become profitable or shut down. But many of them can fall back on a third choice as well: cash in chips with government cronies. As might be expected, this third option is not without its complications.

For example, shortly after the Crash of 2008, Alfa Bank, led by economic oligarch, Mikhail Fridman, sought repayment of a $650 million loan from a holding company, Basic Element, owned by another oligarch, Oleg Deripaska. On hearing this, Deripaska called Dimitry Medvedev, the then Russian president. Medvedev told Fridman to back off.[1]

This was not the end of the story. Basic Element had previously laid off many factory workers and owed some of them pay. Vladimir Putin, who preceded and succeeded Medvedev as president and who was then prime minister, staged a media event in which he dragged Deripaska before some of these laid off and unpaid workers and, in full view of state television cameras, proclaimed, "I wanted the authors of what happened [to these workers] to see it with their own eyes."

Turning to Deripaska directly, he added menacingly, "You have made thousands of [workers] hostage to your ambition, your lack of professionalism, and perhaps your greed."[2]

Was Deripaska about to lose his company? Was he in danger of being sent to prison? Would he be treated like Mikhail Khodorkovsky, another "oligarch" who had offended Putin by supporting democracy and opposition political parties in Russia? No, there was not the least danger of any of this happening.

The dressing down was just for the cameras and no doubt carefully rehearsed. Deripaska was on friendly terms with both Medvedev and Putin, and at that very moment was being bailed out by a state-owned bank, which would also support new stock issuance by the company. Even Alfa's loan would be paid, so Fridman too would be happy.

What Medvedev and Putin got in return, or had gotten at some earlier time from Deripaska, we do not know. But we can guess. Stories have circulated in Russia about how a business "friend" of Putin's has siphoned off hundreds of millions in "charitable" contributions from Russian companies, totaling billions, in order to create off-shore accounts for Putin and also build him what is alleged to be a billion dollar villa on the Black Sea.[3]

This is only one of Putin's lavish residences. He enjoys 20 in all, along with four yachts, countless cars, helicopters, and airplanes, one of which has an $18 million cabin with a $75,000 toilet.[4] Meanwhile the president reports total personal income of $113,000 a year. In all, including 250,000 personnel involved in personal security, the cost of maintaining Putin is believed to total $5 billion a year.[5]

Russian reformer Yegor Gaidar said about the Putin regime: "A self-serving state . . . oppresses . . . society, . . . destroys . . . it and in the end destroys itself."[6]

He died mysteriously in 2009 at age 53.

The Russian state no longer claims ownership of the economy, as it did in Soviet days. How much better to control it without having to take direct responsibility for any of its failures? But there are few boundaries between private and public. Businessmen depend on the state for favors. The state siphons off whatever money it needs or wants, either for political or personal use. As much as possible, it is all done behind closed doors. If control of money and media does not produce the right election result, ballots can be stuffed, also as discretely as possible. And opponents can be intimidated or if necessary beaten, jailed, or killed.

Although Russia may be the "poster boy" for cronyism among the larger national economies today, there are many other vivid examples. Respected economic columnist Larry Kudlow has written that "the Communists in China have adopted deregulated free market capitalism."[7]

He must have been joking.

The Chinese banking system is perennially insolvent, because of bad loans to government cronies, but is always rescued with new cash created by the central bank. The whole country lurches from government-financed bubble to bubble. Stimulus program funds, also in large part generated by the central bank, have been used by state-owned companies to buy private rivals.[8] If this essentially corrupt system finally implodes, as is likely, the entire world will feel its effects, thanks to China's central role in world trade, by far larger than Russia's.

In South America, cronyism has taken deep root, but the most tragic example may be Argentina. Before Juan Perón introduced his own brand of fascism in the 1940s, the country's income per head rivaled that of the United States. Waves of European immigrants came to the country seeking a better life. As Alan Beattie has noted, "The millions of emigrant Italians and Irish feeling poverty at home at the end of the 19th century were torn between two destinations: Buenos Aires or New York."[9] Sixty years later, Argentine income per head had fallen to less than 20% of the US figure.

Given Argentina's natural riches and other advantages, the decline is almost entirely attributable to rampant crony capitalism, which has only gotten worse with time. In 2002, the government defaulted on its global debts. In 2010, it seized private pension monies, and channeled some of these funds to private sector cronies, allegedly to build housing. In 2012, it rewrote rules for the central bank to give itself unlimited use of national reserve funds.

Friends of the government buy a dollar for 4.5 pesos, while others pay 6, if they can get a dollar at all. Taxes are suffocating and on the rise. Economic statistics are all so cooked that the International Monetary Fund has officially criticized them and international publications like *The Economist* refuse to run them. Inflation, always a threat despite government cover-ups, is surging along with unemployment, but Argentine economists are fined for even releasing projections. The government commandeers television whenever it likes and otherwise restricts what is said or shown.

Meanwhile the recent rulers of Argentina, first Nestor and then his wife Cristina Kirchner, have grown rich, principally through land and hotel deals in their native province. When Mr. Kirchner was governor there, he bought at least one piece of land from a town government. An unknown number of purchases were financed by a bank that had been privatized and sold to a family friend. What happened to the proceeds of the privatization sales, including a large oil company, remains a mystery.[10]

Zimbabwe too was once considered a breadbasket, in this case of Africa, but in the 2000s began to suffer mass starvation. The principal reason was that President Robert Mugabe promised land reform, but actually gave the once rich farms to his cronies. At about the same time, everything was price controlled, often below the cost of production. The Central Bank was printing unlimited numbers of Zimbabwean dollars, so that by 2008 prices were rising 98% a day. Property and market values plunged by at least 99%, but it was hard to say for sure, because there were no buyers. While these events were unfolding, Mugabe railed against "greedy entrepreneurs, ruthless markets, and the forces of globalization."[11]

Russia, China, Argentina, and Zimbabwe are all extreme examples of crony capitalism, and therefore useful in defining what we mean by the term. At the same time, they are by no means isolated cases. Most of the world today is crony capitalist to one degree or another.

The kind of political and economic system exemplified by these four countries has clear roots in the "national socialism" developed by Mussolini in Italy and copied by Hitler in Germany. But it was by no means a 20th century invention. The earlier monarchies of Europe and Asia worked in a not dissimilar way. Indeed it may be argued that cronyism is as old as recorded human history and has always been the dominant system.

This is precisely why the human race has made so little progress in overcoming poverty. For most of human history, there has been no economic growth at all. People born poor died poor. Whenever economic capital began to be accumulated, it was generally stolen by rulers or their friends or allies.

The British economist John Maynard Keynes observed in the 1930s that only one treasure trove, taken by the English privateer Sir Francis Drake in the 16th century from a Spanish galleon, the *Golden Hind*, invested at 3%, would have equaled the entire English economy by the time he wrote. Such is the power of compound interest from a successful business or financial investment. But for most of human history, large-scale investments have been unthinkable. It has not been safe to make them. Treasure was to be spent or hidden.

By the beginning of the 18th century, the world was just as impoverished as it had always been. But very gradually, in some countries, especially in Britain and the newly formed United States, governments learned to be less greedy, to avoid killing the goose of enterprise that laid the golden eggs. Reforms, especially reforms that freed some prices from government control, were achieved, the so-called industrial revolution began, and poverty began to decline, especially by the 19th century.

Even then, reform was limited, cronyism remained strong, and millions remained in poverty despite advances. Outside the more reformed and thus more advanced countries, people remained uncertain about their next meal. How could it be otherwise when their economy was run on crony capitalist lines—principally for the benefit of rulers and powerful allied special interests?

2

Crony Capitalism in America

THE UNITED STATES, Europe, and Japan are some of the advanced economies that benefited from the 18th and 19th century reforms of the old crony capitalism. They have nothing in common with Russia, China, Argentina, or Zimbabwe. Or do they?

By 2012, the US government was financing most of its $1.2 trillion deficit by "borrowing" from its own central bank, the US Federal Reserve. It was thus "borrowing" more from itself than from foreign lenders such as Japan or China. This money printing had not reached peak Zimbabwean levels. But once a country starts using newly printed money to pay its bills, it is not easy to control the process. The 28 recorded national hyper-inflations (prices advancing 50% or more a month) of 20th century world history[12] attest to this.

During the US bubble years (about 1995–2008) fueled by all the money printing, political and financial scandals increased apace. Why? One explanation is that government and private interests were "part-nering" more; the line between the two was increasingly blurred. Looked at one way, this meant more government control of private interests. Looked at another way, it meant the opposite: more control of government by private interests.

Economic textbooks refer somewhat misleadingly to "public" and "private" sectors. Before the rapid expansion of the federal government by the George W. Bush and Obama administrations, the public sector (including federal, state, and local) was thought to represent about a third of the economy. The nonprofit sector, often overlooked, accounted for another 10%. This math suggested that just a bit over half of the economy was "private, for-profit." But taking into account companies and other organizations that are directly or indirectly run by government, it becomes clear that most of the economy is in the "public" sphere.

The term Government Sponsored Enterprise (GSE) is often applied to so-called private enterprises that have been founded by government and still enjoy public support of one kind or another. Pre-eminent examples include the mortgage giants Fannie Mae and Freddie Mac.

It is appropriate, however, to apply the term GSE more broadly to include:

- The defense industry (sells mostly to the government);
- Healthcare, drugs, housing, banking, finance, agriculture, food, autos, broadcasting, railroads, trucking, airlines, education (closely regulated, subsidized, price supported, protected, or cartelized by government);
- Law and accounting (expanded through government regulation and allowed to earn enormous fees in areas such as medical malpractice law);
- Unions (exempted from anti-trust law and favored in many other ways);
- Other niche organizations such as the American Association for Retired Persons (AARP) (ostensibly exists to influence government, although it has become in effect a large business conglomerate aided and assisted by government).

It is clear enough why all these "private" firms and organizations reach out and try to ally themselves with public officials. They may be looking for:

- Sales
- Favorable regulations

- Exemption from regulation
- Regulation that discourages new or small competitors
- Access to credit
- Access to cheap credit
- Loan guarantees
- Monopoly status
- Extension of monopoly status (patents and copyrights)
- Noncompetitive bidding or contracts
- Subsidies
- Bail-outs
- Promise of a future bail-out (which reduces current cost of credit)
- Protection from competitors, domestic or foreign
- Favorable price restrictions
- Targeted tax breaks

Public officials in turn have a list of what they want:

- Campaign contributions
- Direct campaign assistance
- Indirect campaign assistance
- Assistance with "messaging"
- Money (illegal if takes the form of a bribe, but not necessarily in other cases, e.g. assistance with a loan or access to a "sweetheart" investment)

- Support from "foundations" related to campaign contributors
- Regulatory fees to support agency jobs
- Jobs for friends, constituents, or eventually themselves
- Travel, entertainment, other "freebies"
- Power, control, and deference

The alliances and relationships formed between public officials and private interests may at first seem counter-intuitive. A company may give more campaign money to a potentially hostile legislator than to a friendly one, in order to forestall trouble. For example, Senators Chuck Schumer (D-New York) and Harry Reid (D-Nevada) received large contributions from Wall Street hedge funds in 2007–2009 in an effort to head off a plan by House Democrats to tax the funds' "carried interest" profits at regular income rather than capital gains rates. As a result, Democrats raised twice as much from hedge funds in the 2008 cycle and in 2009 as Republicans.[13]

Uganda dictator and ruthless killer Idi Amin once observed that "in politics there are no permanent enemies or permanent friends." This is indeed evident in what are often shifting alliances among private interests and public officials. On most occasions, the US Chamber of Commerce (representing business interests) competes with large trade unions for favor on Capitol Hill, in the White House, or in government agencies. But if budget cuts threaten spending on highways or mass transit, the antagonists join forces to stop it. They have also agreed about bail-outs for banks, bail-outs for General Motors and Chrysler, and stimulus bills.

Many of these players are not even US citizens. Much of the money newly minted by the Fed after the 2008 Crash went to support foreign banks. An MSNBC headline read: "Wind at Their Backs: Powerful Democrats Help Chinese Energy Firm Chase Stimulus Money." The article explained how Senator Reid (D-Nevada) received campaign money from a Chinese project's backers. Although it is not widely known, foreign nationals may legally contribute to US federal and state campaigns, so long as they hold a green card.

After the 2008 Crash, commentator Michael Barone noted that many people expected US voters to turn against "Big Business" and "market solutions" in favor of more "Big Government."[14] But it is difficult to draw such distinctions when Big Business, Big Finance, Big Labor, Big Law, and Big Government all merge together into a single conglomerated entity, one that seems devoted to its own welfare rather than the public good.

The position of rich people is always ambiguous, but especially so under such circumstances. In the past, they had generally been characterized as predators and parasites (the unfavorable Marxist view) or sage investors and job creators (the favorable view). Now these stereotypes were further complicated by the source of the wealth.

Many of the new mega rich of the 1990s and 2000s got their wealth through their government connections or by understanding how government worked. This was especially apparent on Wall Street, which had first use of all the new money printed by the Fed and which had gotten very rich under President George W. Bush, then even richer under President Obama.* Economist George Reisman, author of *Capitalism*, a brilliant 1,000-page defense of its title subject, regarded rich government cronies as "aberrations,"[15] but in the bubble years they seemed no longer the exception, rather the rule.

This was all the more regrettable because, in a crony capitalist system, the huge gains of the few really do come at the expense of the many. There was an irony here. Perhaps Marx had been right all along! It was just that he was describing a crony capitalist, not a free price system, and his most devoted followers set up a system in the Soviet Union that was cronyist to the core.

A free price system is not what economists call a zero sum game, in which existing wealth simply changes hands. On the contrary, it continually creates new wealth, large amounts of new wealth, and everybody

---

* Wall Street made as much profit in the first three years under Obama as in the prior eight years under Bush.

potentially benefits. A cronyist system by contrast is a negative sum game; it destroys what wealth exists without creating much new wealth to replenish it.

A few years after the Crash of 2008, Sol Sanders, columnist for a "conservative" newspaper, wrote that President Obama should "begin weekly meetings in closed session with a group of recognized private-sector leaders to brainstorm recovery strategy and tactics." No worse advice can be imagined. Such a meeting—behind closed doors no less—would not be a recipe for job creation. It would be a recipe for more of the cronyism that has already destroyed millions of jobs and brought the economy to the brink of utter ruin.

Whom would the president invite? Which of the powerful private economic interests that despise open, honest, competitive markets and conspire with government to protect what they have and prevent any change threatening them? Would it be the head of the president's outside economic council, the CEO of General Electric, which just happens to have been rescued by the government and is also a major government contractor? The heads of the major banks that were bailed out and are still being bailed out by the Federal Reserve? The heads of drug companies whose monopoly is jealously guarded by the Food and Drug Administration (FDA), an agency that drug companies directly fund? The head of Government Motors, aka General Motors?

Such access to government leaders in a crony capitalist economy is worth a lot. How much? Here is one measure. When word of Timothy Geithner's selection to be President Obama's treasury secretary leaked, the stocks of companies considered close to him immediately jumped by an average of 15%.[16] This is hardly surprising. Geithner had already saved many of these companies billions of dollars when, as president of the New York Fed, he had quietly vetoed a plan for banks to take losses on their contracts with failed insurer AIG, and had instead decided that the government, that is the taxpayers, would absorb the loss.[17]

18th century economist Adam Smith warned that

> people of the same trade seldom meet together, even for merriment and diversion, but the conversation ends in a conspiracy against the public, or in some contrivance to raise prices.

How much worse, then, if these merchants are meeting behind closed doors with the president of the US or secretary of the Treasury? The Obama White House presumably understands the potential value of such meetings, because it first offered to provide full logs of all White House visitors, pointedly excluding the first nine months, and then began scheduling lobbyist visits outside the White House, at the nearby Jackson Place offices, where the promise of logs was deemed not to apply, or even at coffee houses.[18]

An earlier secretary of the Treasury, William Simon, had written that

> I watched with incredulity as businessmen ran to the government in every crisis, whining for handouts or protection from the very competition that has made this system so productive.... Always, such gentlemen proclaimed their devotion to free enterprise.... Their own case [however] ... was always unique and ... justified [an exception].[19]

Today's deal-making between private interests (not just businesses) and government goes far beyond the kind of special pleading that Simon describes. It involves what "public interest" economists broadly call "rent-seeking," pursuing special deals and advantages of every kind. In most cases, the deals require some further interference with free prices, interference that makes some people much richer and society as a whole much poorer.

Humorist P. J. O'Rourke says about this:

> I don't mind America becoming a third world country.... The troubled economy will soon be a thing of the past. Once we've got third world-style full-blown business [, non-business,] and government corruption, there won't be an economy.[20]

Part 2

Crony Politicians

3

Pay to Play:
A Capitol Hill
Primer

I

F YOU ARE a politician looking for campaign contributions, a few basic rules apply:

1. Make laws and regulations as complicated and
   vague as possible. Take the tax code for example. The more complex and vague it is, the easier to trade special deals and provisions for campaign money or assistance. This is the primary
   reason that the tax code keeps getting longer and
   longer, ever more dense and impenetrable, even
   though anyone can see that a simpler and more
   transparent system would raise more money and
   immeasurably help the economy.

2. Complicated and vague laws also directly benefit lawyers, accountants, and tax preparation firms, all good sources of campaign money.

3. The more complicated and vague legislation is created, the more powerful special interests will be interested in having "friends" in government. When the Constitution was first ratified, there were only three federal crimes: treason, counterfeiting, and piracy. Today no one is sure how many federal crimes there are, but a 2007 study estimated 4,450.[21]

Even if laws were not so numerous, complex, and vague, large companies today regard close ties to key government figures as a very necessary kind of insurance policy, and they are right to do so. For example, why were Goldman Sachs executives never prosecuted for Senate testimony under oath following the Crash of 2008, when some objective observers thought they had clearly perjured themselves? Was it because of campaign contributions? Because of payments made to the law firm where the Attorney General, Eric Holder, had worked and would presumably return to work? For whatever reason, Goldman Sachs executives got away with it, even after a Senator sent the dossier to the Justice Department. We shall return to this question in a later chapter devoted to Goldman Sachs.

4. When crafting a bill, leave as much as possible to be filled in by regulatory agencies. The Affordable Care

Act (Obamacare), the Dodd-Frank Act "reform-ing" Wall Street, and the Food Safety Act of 2011 are all good examples. This is advantageous because it means that the bill will take shape over many years, and special interests will keep mak-ing campaign donations in hope of influencing the regulations long after the statute has passed. As we shall see in a later chapter, the Dodd-Frank Wall Street reform bill, 2,000 pages long, was expected to require five years of regulation writing, which would fill hundreds of thousands of pages.[22]

5. Whenever possible, provide for waivers and exemp-tions from new legislation, but only on request to regulatory agencies. This means that friends can be rewarded. For example, President Obama's Stim-ulus Act had a "buy American" provision, but it could be waived on request. His Affordable Care Act also provided for waivers, which in the first year mostly went to union and other supporters.

6. If through an oversight, an exemption or waiver is not included in the statute, the next best thing is to include it as a regulatory rule. Thus, after the Dodd-Frank Act was passed requiring hedge funds to register and report to the government, a rule was written to exempt funds handling only "family money" (however defined). George Soros, a major Obama campaign contributor who had earlier called for regulation of hedge funds

under Dodd-Frank, promptly returned non-family money to investors so that he could claim the exemption for his own fund.[23]

7. Reward your friends but also punish your foes. For example, in 2009, Congressman James L. Oberstar (D-Minnesota) slipped a 230-word provision into legislation re-authorizing the Federal Aviation Administration. The provision would have moved regulation of the Federal Express Company from the Railway Labor Act to the National Labor Relations Act. This was a long-time objective of FedEx's competitor, United Parcel Service (UPS) and its Teamster Union allies, which thought the move would "hobble" FedEx and help the unionized UPS.

Not surprisingly Bloomberg News reported that the UPS political action committee has "given more money to federal lawmakers than any other company over two decades" and that Mr. Oberstar had received $77,900 from UPS employees. The Teamsters over the same period had given $86,500 to Oberstar.[24] In 2009, the Oberstar maneuver was blocked in the Senate, but that may not displease the congressman. So long as the issue remains unresolved, UPS and the Teamsters are likely to stay firmly allied with him.

8. If you cannot directly punish your foes, try to intimidate them. For example, in 2011, the Obama

Administration threatened to issue an executive order requiring any company bidding on a government contract to list prior political contributions. The implicit threat was that if you have donated to the opposite party, you will not get the contract. The leak of this plan was timed to chill donations to the other party just as the presidential campaign was getting under way.[25]

Another example was Senator Dick Durbin's October, 2011, speech describing Bank of America's new $5 a month debit card charge as an "outrage" and encouraging customers to leave the bank. This was a rather extreme tactic in that the Senator was in effect trying to create a "run" on a major bank, that is, a sudden withdrawal of deposits, something that the government has tried to prevent since the Great Depression. In this case, the Bank dropped the new fee (knowing it could recoup with other, less visible fees) and also probably made a private decision to increase, not decrease, its contribution to Senator Durbin.[26] Senator Durbin would be unlikely to receive $14.6 million from financial firms, as his close colleague senator Charles Schumer (D-New York) has over the years, but then Schumer "represents" Wall Street, and always fights for what it wants, while Durbin threatens Wall Street, a less remunerative but still robust fundraising strategy.[27]

9. When punishing, intimidating, or indirectly seeking campaign contributions from "the other side," look for issues that will affect as many of them as possible. A classic example of this was President Obama's proposal (American Jobs Act of 2011) to allow the unemployed to sue employers for discrimination when they have been turned down for a job. This sent a clear message: business employers had better stay in touch with the administration (direct campaign contributions or contributions raised by lobbyists) as the presidential race was getting underway.[28]

10. Don't always aim to punish or intimidate foes. Sometimes it is better to placate them. For example, when Congressional Democrats offered a restrictive campaign finance bill in June 2010, they decided, after consultation with the White House, to exempt their foe, The National Rifle Association, in order to forestall the powerful NRA's opposition. In order to camouflage this move a bit, they also exempted an ally, the Sierra Club, and the more non-partisan Humane Society.[29]

11. Whenever passing legislation, look for a chance to create a role for friends. For example, when Washington bailed out Wall Street during the Crash of 2008, different pieces of legislation authorized hiring consultants from—where else?—Wall Street to advise government agencies and monitor

bail-out activities. Black Rock, whose CEO Larry Fink is especially well connected, and which is well known for its political contributions, won the lion's share of the business, without competitive bidding or indeed any disclosure of how the selection was made,[30] although other firms benefited as well.

12. When directly subsidizing private interests, it is helpful to create a confusing array of overlapping programs. That way, favored donors can win multiple subsidies without being noticed. For example, the same company can be directed to the Defense Department, Agriculture Department, Energy Department, and Small Business Administration for loan guarantees and also pick up a grant from the Stimulus Program.

13. Try to keep government contracts on a "no-bid" basis. For example, a company controlled by a major Obama donor won a $433 million no-bid contract on an experimental smallpox remedy, although it is uncertain whether smallpox even still exists.[31]

14. Rely on lobbyists to find campaign donors and do not look too hard at the ones they produce. Recent investigations have uncovered a lobbyist directly reimbursing donors, which is illegal, or indirectly reimbursing them by paying inflated fees for vague services. Super-lobbyist Paul

Maglinocchetti was convicted and sent to prison for these practices in 2011.[32]

15. Help to create monopolies and cartels, e.g. the National Football League, other sports franchises, patent-based businesses such as drug companies, securities rating services, license-restricted businesses such as medicine, and labor unions, among many others. Cartel owners can be relied on to support their cartel status by making plentiful political donations.

16. Keep in mind that large companies, even when they are not granted cartel status by government, still benefit from dense regulations, mandates, and assorted entitlements. All of these legal complexities discourage new competitors, especially small companies which have not grown big enough to afford an army of accountants, lawyers, and political advisors. As *New York Times* columnist David Brooks has said,

> What do corporations, when they go to Washington, . . . want? One, they want subsidies. Two, they want to crush small businesses who are hoping to compete with them by erecting regulatory hurdles. . . . They want to stifle competition.[33]

17. Whenever possible snag a seat (or even better a chairmanship) of a Committee with authority

over taxes or other money matters. A dispute over the use of rum taxes filled New York Democratic Congressman Charles B. Rangle's campaign coffers in 2009 because he chaired the tax-writing House Ways and Means Committee.[34]

18. Condition your support of a major bill on the inclusion of a specific provision, often unrelated to the bill in question, favoring a friendly special interest supporter or constituent group. Senator Harry Reid (D-Nevada), Senate Majority Leader, said about the Affordable Care Act (Obamacare) in December 2009: "There's 100 Senators here.... If they don't have something in [the bill] important to them, it doesn't speak well of them." [35]

19. Completely unrelated provisions favoring a particular constituent are usually termed earmarks. Thousands of them may be included in a single major bill, especially a "must pass" appropriations bill. The most famous recent example was the Alaskan "bridge to nowhere." Sometimes these maneuvers do not go as intended. In 2009, House Democratic Whip James E. Clyburn (D-South Carolina) thought he had successfully earmarked $100,000 for a library in Jamestown, SC, but found that through a clerical error the money had gone to Jamestown, CA, a town that does not even have a library. Following efforts to end earmarks, it has become more popular to designate nonprofits as

the recipient—since nonprofits are excluded from the proposed bans. In some cases, this has resulted in the creation of new nonprofits to receive funding that had already been requested for companies or other private interests creating the nonprofit.[36] In other instances, earmarks have funded projects close to property owned by the legislator.[37]

20. Use judgment when agreeing to help campaign donors or powerful special interests. Consider how it will appear if made public. For example, it was not wise for the US Department of Veteran Affairs in 2009 to approve Prudential's withholding of lump sum life insurance payments to families of soldiers killed in combat (replacing them with retained asset accounts, on which the company continued to earn interest). Making money off fallen soldiers was going too far, and this was also too crude an example of crony capitalism. Or, perhaps it was not. The policy has not been changed, and a federal lawsuit will take years to unfold.[38]

21. If necessary, stretch or even break the law. For example, the Obama Administration told Defense contractors not to announce layoffs prior to the election of 2012. In return, the administration promised to reimburse the firms from government funds if waiting to give notice led to higher severance costs, even though no legislation authorized this.[39]

22. Although federal contracts or stimulus grants are tangible rewards for donations, less tangible rewards are also important. Major Obama donor and "bundler" (collector of donations) Donald H. Gips received $13.8 million in federal stimulus money for his firm, Level 3 Communications. But he was also named ambassador to South Africa.[40]

Other donors have been invited to high level administration "briefings" or White House events, in addition to being given access to high officials. President Obama hosted an end-of-Ramadan dinner to reward Muslim donors, a novel addition to the usual St. Patricks' Day gathering, state dinners, intimate gatherings in the White House movie theater, or even more intimate golf outings or basketball games.[41] The president was occasionally criticized for playing too much golf; but the golf games were important fundraising opportunities.

When running for president in 2007, then Senator Obama attacked "the cynics and the lobbyists and the special interests who've turned our government into a game only they can afford to play. . . . They write the checks and you get stuck with the bill." In keeping with this, he promised to accept public funding of his presidential campaign, even though it would legally restrict his private fundraising. But when he saw an opportunity to out-fundraise his Republican opponent, Senator McCain, he quickly broke his promise and dispensed with public funding so that he could raise an unlimited amount of private money.

4

Political ATMs: Fannie and Freddie

CONVENTIONAL WISDOM BLAMES the US housing bubble of the 2000s on Wall Street greed. This is only a half-truth. When government serves free drinks by printing money, driving interest rates down, and overspending, Wall Street tends to get drunk. This is very convenient for government because, when the hangover comes, the average person will blame the drunk, not the bartender. This happened each time a bubble popped, at the end of the 1920s, the end of the 1990s, and the end of the recent housing bubble.

Throughout the housing bubble, the Federal Reserve, by far the most powerful government agency, sought to provide cheap mortgages by driving interest rates down, generally with the help of other central banks. By holding the Fed Funds Rate below the rate of inflation for three years, it virtually made a free gift of money to those with the clout and the collateral to get it. These initial borrowers then made the money available to other borrowers, especially to consumers for housing loans.

The US government had already greased the housing industry by making mortgage interest tax deductible and eliminating most capital gains taxes on homes. It also provided loan guarantees through the Federal Housing Administration (FHA) and its own cheap mortgages through both the Federal Home Loan Banks and the private/public entities Fannie Mae and Freddie Mac. The government's Department of Housing and Urban Development mandated that Fannie and Freddie invest what became 50% of assets in lower-end mortgages, including, if necessary, unqualified mortgages, the ones that later blew up.[42] The federal government has no fewer than 160 housing programs in all[43]; each of them contributed in some measure to blowing up the bubble.

Even the Federal Reserve joined the effort to get more mortgage loans out to what were often unqualified buyers. While HUD pressured Fannie and Freddie, the Fed told the banks it regulated that "discrimination may be observed when a lender's underwriting policies contain arbitrary or outdated criteria that effectively disqualify many urban or lower-income minority applicants."[44] Examples of "outdated criteria" included exclusion of welfare or unemployment insurance income and consideration of past repayment history.

By the end of 2007, government-sponsored mortgages accounted for 81% of all the mortgage loans made in the US,[45] and by 2010 this had risen to 100%. Many of these loans during the 2000s were developed by shady "bucket shops" that, when shut down, just reopened next door under a new name.[46] During 2008, Fannie Mae also developed the Home Saver program. This enabled defaulting homeowners to borrow additional money to cover the arrears in their mortgage payments.

Although ostensibly designed to help struggling homeowners, the new Home Saver loans meant that none of the original loans had to be considered in default. More importantly, none of them had to be written off or at least not immediately written off. It is true that many of the new loans themselves fell into default and had to be written off, but the write-offs were small compared to the original loans that could be kept on the books for a while longer. In this and other creative ways, Fannie executives kept kicking the can (of mortgage defaults) down the road a bit further into the future.[47]

Official government propaganda touted home ownership as the American dream. No one paid attention to studies showing that countries and regions with the highest home ownership also had the highest unemployment rate. Why? Because home ownership makes it difficult for workers to move to where the jobs are, especially to where the best jobs for their particular skills are.[48] This was finally noticed after the housing crash.

Democratic politicians especially liked Fannie and Freddie. They exempted them from state and local taxes and some Securities and Exchange Commission (SEC) requirements and also gave them implied government backing for their bonds. They fought off Bush administration efforts to regulate them more, even after it became apparent that both firms had issued false accounting statements. They also saw nothing wrong with Fannie and Freddie borrowing $60 for each $1 of capital, much more leverage than even Wall Street used. At FHA, the leverage rate reached an eye-popping 840 to 1 by 2012.

Representative Barney Frank (D-Massachusetts), chair of the US House Financial Services Committee, said that fears of a looming crisis were "exaggerated." His counterpart in the Senate, Christopher Dodd (D-Connecticut), chair of the Banking Committee, agreed.[49] As late as July 2008, Dodd said that "[Fannie and Freddie] are fundamentally sound and

strong; there is no reason for the reaction we're getting."[50] Before the end of that year, both companies
had collapsed and been refinanced by the government.

By June 2011, the federal government had spent
$130 billion bailing out Fannie and Freddie, and
the Congressional Budget Office estimated that
another $187 billion would be needed to restore
their solvency.[51] By March 2012, the loss to date had
risen to $183 billion. The Obama Administration
was also pressing for more forgiveness of loans. This
would help the homeowners of course, but also the
big banks, which often held second mortgages atop
the Fannie- or Freddie-guaranteed first mortgages.
These second mortgages, currently worthless, would
become valuable if some or all of the first mortgages
could be written off.[52]

The financial condition of the Federal Housing
Administration received less notice, but behind its
lax accounting standards, it was deeply insolvent as
well. Choosing simply to disregard the hole it was
in, it kept piling on the loan guarantees, tripling its
book in 2008–2010. Congress as usual made things
worse by increasing the maximum single loan guarantee to $729,750 before the crisis; FHA responded
by moving to guarantee loans on luxury Manhattan
apartments featuring concierge service, pet spas, mas-
sage rooms, and rooftop lounges. Down payment
required?—only 3.5% of purchase price. Loans were

even available where 70% of the building remained unsold, which meant the project was not yet viable.[53] Post crisis, the limit on jumbo loan guarantees was reduced—to $625,500.[54]

Prior to 2008, Frank worried that any attempt to rein in Fannie and Freddie would make housing less "affordable," presumably for people of modest means. He did not explain how jumbo loan guarantees fit into his goal of helping those with less. Nor did he explain how soaring home values, fueled by cheap government money, made homes more affordable.

By 2006, cheap credit had doubled the price of the average house in less than ten years.[55] By then, the housing bubble had spread around the world and become the largest and most universal bubble in economic history. The 1920s bubble in the US led to a total debt to gross domestic product ratio of 185% by 1928. The housing bubble led to a total US debt to GDP ratio of 357% by 2008.[56]

What nobody mentioned throughout the debate about Fannie and Freddie was how convenient their supposedly private (but actually public) status was for politicians. As private companies, they could make campaign contributions through their employees and their PACs (Political Action Committees). Their "foundations" could also provide "soft" funding for a host of political purposes. As *Forbes* magazine publisher Steve Forbes noted in August 2008:

The two most mammoth political power-houses in America today are Fannie Mae and Freddie Mac. Their lobbying muscle makes Arnold Schwarzenegger look like a 90-pound weakling. Directly and indirectly, they employ legions of ex-pols to help them [and their friends] on the Hill. They hand out largesse of one sort or another to any pol who matters and is willing to take it. Fannie Mae's "charitable" operations have field people in virtually every congressional district.

These monsters are fiercely resistant to any change affecting their ability to tap Uncle Sam's ATM at will while privatizing profits and socializing losses.[57]

Fannie's "non-political" money even went to ACORN, the group charged in 2008 with voter fraud.[58] Altogether, excluding "charitable" gifts, Fannie spent $170 million on lobbying from 1998–2007 and $19.3 million on campaign contributions from 1990. The largest sum during the 2006–2008 electoral cycle went to Senate Banking Committee Chairman Dodd, and the second largest to then Senator Obama.[59]

Senator Dodd was the second largest recipient of funds (in this case exceeded by President Obama) from a political action committee (PAC) organized by Countrywide Financial, a leading subprime mortgage lender.[60] He was also recipient of two mortgages from Countrywide's VIP program that waived points and other fees. Later Dodd stated that he did not realize he was getting special treatment and refinanced the loans elsewhere.

A sweetheart Countrywide loan also went to Jim Johnson, Fannie executive and Obama advisor. When the chairman of the House Oversight and Government Reform Committee, Edolphus Towns (D-New York), issued a subpoena to gain access to Countrywide records, he exempted his own records, which would have revealed two such loans.[61] President Obama did not receive a Countrywide loan, but there are questions about how he bought his own Chicago home on a double lot. Tony Rezko, a developer, political operator, and campaign donor now in jail, put up the cash for the second lot, and Northern Trust provided a discounted rate mortgage as confirmed by the Federal Election Commission.[62]

Vice President Joe Biden also seems to have made some "sharp" real estate deals. He sold a luxurious home in Delaware for $1.2 million to mortgage firm MBNA Vice Chairman John Cochran at full listed price during a weak market. MBNA also hired Biden's son. With profits from the house sale, Biden then bought a 4.2-acre lakefront lot from a real estate developer, Keith Stoltz, who had paid the same price five years earlier, and thus did not make a profit.[63]

Private/public entities like Fannie and Freddie were not just a ready source of funds for politicians. They also represented an ideal way to reward cronies, who could in turn be counted on for more political donations and fundraising. President Obama's first two chiefs of staff, Rahm Emanuel and Bill Daley, had each been appointed to the Fannie board by President Clinton. New directors at that time received $380,000 in stock and options plus a $20,000 annual fee. It was estimated that Emanuel earned $46,000 an hour for his 14 month Fannie service.

Clinton's choice for Fannie CEO, Franklin Raines, took away $90 million in pay and stock option gains, in part because of misleading accounting practices. Obama advisor James Johnson took only $21 million. For 2009–2010, the chief executives of Fannie and Freddie got a combined $17 million, even as these organizations were being bailed out. The top six executives got $35 million over the same period.[64]

After the size of the Fannie/Freddie/FHA financial hole became clear, US Treasury Undersecretary Jeffrey A. Goldstein acknowledged that "the current structure of the government's role in the housing-finance market is unsustainable and unacceptable."[65] Did this mean there was an intention of actually reducing the government role? No. The last time anyone heard from the government about its plans for FHA, Fannie, and Freddie was when a group of Wall

Street managers spoke privately to Treasury Secretary Paulson in the fall of 2008 and apparently got inside information that the government would stand behind all their liabilities.[66]

Meanwhile, crisis or no crisis, it was business as usual at the mortgage giants. In 2011, Fannie and Freddie sent 87 employees to party in Chicago at the Mortgage Bankers Association Conference. Freddie was a platinum level sponsor of the event, which cost $80,000 in taxpayer money. Fannie was only a gold sponsor, which cost $60,000.[67]

Possibly looking at what Fannie and Freddie had been, and might be again, Senator John Kerry (D-Massachusetts) introduced a bill in March 2011 to create a $10 billion infrastructure bank, an idea first introduced by Senator Dodd in 2007 and endorsed by President Obama. The bank would use its $10 billion to seed a supposed $640 billion of infrastructure projects such as roads and bridges, all fully guaranteed by the federal government. Not surprisingly both the AFL-CIO and the US Chamber of Commerce liked this idea. But a new financial slush fund of that size, organized in a way that would allow campaign contributions from its employees, must have especially appealed to the politicians who supported it. Just think of all the "friends" that could be made, all the allies rewarded, all the campaign funds raised with $640 billion at the government's disposal?[68]

5

Honey Pots 1:
The Recovery Act
("Stimulus")

THE 2009 STIMULUS PROGRAM (Recovery Act) is by now a widely chronicled example of crony capitalism, but some of the details are still worth recounting:

1. President Obama said the bill would be free of earmarks and after passage claimed that it was "clean." It was not. House Speaker Nancy Pelosi got a wetlands provision for her district. Senate Majority Leader Harry Reid put in $2 billion for a high-speed rail line from Los Angeles to Las Vegas. Although the House version of the bill included nothing for this project, the "compromise" between House

($0) and Senate ($2 billion) in the joint House/ Senate conference committee was to increase the rail project to $8 billion!

2. The bill also contained unrelated provisions inserted by other legislators or the administration, including $246 million in targeted tax breaks for Hollywood, $198 million for Filipino World War II veterans, many not resident in the US, and a requirement that all medical records be made electronic with no consumer opt-out for privacy.

   The inclusion of these unrelated items was not surprising. Even the earlier TARP bill passed by Congress during the Crash of 2008 as an "emergency" crisis measure had contained unrelated provisions favoring rum producers, companies operating in American Samoa (explanation: one of these, Sunkist, is based in Speaker Nancy Pelosi's district), auto race tracks, even a requirement that medical insurance cover mental health.[69]

3. 40% of the stimulus bill spending was targeted for 2011 or later. This might seem puzzling for an act passed in 2009 as another emergency spending measure, but was clearly intended to provide economic insurance for the 2012 election.

4. By January 2010, the government's own figures showed that jobs allegedly created by the Act, most of them unsustainable, had cost an average of $245,808 each.[70]

5. Districts of Democratic members of Congress received on average 1.6 times as many awards as Republican districts, and twice as much money.[71]

6. Almost 90% of grants went to state or local governments, entities whose jobs are only sustainable over the long run with private tax revenue.[72] Much of this money was really a payoff to public sector unions which were concurrently bankrupting state and local governments. The cash made it possible to keep funding inflated employee benefits in particular. We will discuss this further in a later chapter.

7. Mark Penn, Democratic pollster, received a $6 million contract to work on the Federal Communications Commission's (FCC) digital television readiness campaign. This allegedly created three jobs.[73]

8. The Labor Department awarded $2 million in stimulus contracts to a public relations firm, one of whose tasks was to prepare advertising on "progressive movement" television shows friendly to the administration. Keith Olbermann and Rachel Maddow on MSNBC, a subsidiary of General Electric, whose CEO was also close to the administration, qualified. This money was rated as producing no job.[74]

9. The FCC also used $1 million in stimulus money to hire a firm located in Britain, Sam Knows Ltd.,

to collect data on broadband speeds of Internet Service Providers (ISPs).[75]

10. A $529 million loan guarantee went to an electric car company, Fisker, which produces its cars in Finland. The company was backed by a venture capital firm where former Democratic presidential candidate Al Gore is a partner.[76] Among many challenges faced by the company were safety recalls and the bankruptcy of its battery maker, A123 Systems, which also received stimulus funding.[77]

11. A Government Accountability Office (GAO) study found that stimulus checks totaling $24 billion had been sent to 3,700 recipients who were delinquent in paying federal taxes. In one case, $700,000 went to a construction company with unpaid tax bills and an executive owing hundreds of thousands of dollars from gambling losses.[78]

12. The Department of Commerce gave One Economy Corporation over $28 million to increase fast internet service in areas without it. One Economy then directed $1.5 million to a film production company owned by actor/director, Robert Townsend, and $230,000 was used to produce an internet soap opera. The stated rationale was that the soap opera would create an incentive for people, especially minorities, to use the internet.[79]

13. Billions of dollars of stimulus money went to big companies (DuPont, Duke Energy, etc.) emitting large amounts of air or water pollution. But most of the grants were awarded with an exemption from environmental laws. Below are the departments, the percent exempted from environmental review, and the total dollars spent as of September 30, 2010:[80]

DEPARTMENT	% EXEMPTED FROM ENVIRONMENTAL REVIEW	$ (BILLIONS) AMOUNT SPENT
Agriculture	98.3	22.9
Commerce	63.7	6.8
Defense	88.5	10.8
Energy	98.7	33.0
Health and Human Services	90.4	21.9
Homeland Security	84.0	2.2
Housing and Urban Development	91.6	11.6
Interior	86.4	2.9
Justice	99.7	4.0
Labor	92.9	4.8
State	22.7	0.4
Transportation	95.5	39.4
Treasury	100.0	0.2
Veteran's Affairs	99.3	1.4

Note that these environmental exemptions were provided, not by an environmentally unfriendly administration such as that of George W. Bush, but by an administration that claimed to be the opposite.

14. As the previous table shows, the Department of Energy was second only to Transportation in the size of its Obama stimulus awards. In his book, *Throw Them All Out*, Hoover Institution scholar and Government Accountability Institute founder Peter Schweizer combed through and cross referenced lists of 2008 Obama campaign donors and recipients of Energy Department "green energy" stimulus grants and loans. He found that:

- 71% of the money went to Obama donors
- These donors received $24,783 in stimulus money for every dollar of political campaign contribution[81]

Vice President Joe Biden said during the 2012 presidential campaign that

we're about promoting the private sector. They're [Republicans are] about protecting the privileged sector. . . . Ultimately that's what this election is all about. It's a choice . . . between a system that's rigged and one that's fair.[82]

Contrary to the vice president's claim, in reality both major political parties promote the welfare of special interest donors, usually a different set of donors, but sometimes the same donors who want to play both sides of the fence as a political insurance policy.

15. The Energy Policy Act of 2005 created a Section 1703 loan program for new (not yet commercial) technologies. Few companies took advantage of it. The Stimulus Act grafted a much less restrictive new Section 1705 program onto the older bill. When the loans made under the new Section 1705 began to go bad, President Obama claimed that the program had begun under President Bush, a clear falsehood.[83]

16. Solyndra was the first green energy company funded under Section 1705 (a total of $535 million) and the program's most spectacular failure. It was primarily promoted by Obama donor and fundraiser George Kaiser, a frequent White House visitor who also tried to get the government to buy solar panels from companies like his.[84] Wall Street investment banker Goldman Sachs also touted Solyndra although prudently never invested any money.[85] As the company approached bankruptcy and thereafter, the Internal Revenue Service charged that it was seeking to turn the company's government funded

losses into tax benefits for the owners.[86] Meanwhile company executives, including those who
had overseen the company's collapse, were paid
bonuses.

17. Solyndra claimed that it had been harmed by
unfair Chinese competition, and on this basis,
won assistance of $13,000 for each of its former
workers from the Department of Labor. Other,
less well connected firms, were turned down.[87]

18. There is reason to believe that Chinese solar companies were indeed "dumping" products in the
US at lower than production cost, although it
is doubtful that this was the primary reason for
Solyndra's failure. It is unlikely that the company was ever viable. Despite charges of Chinese "dumping," 60% of green energy grants
went to foreign companies, according to an ABC
News report in 2010.[88] Even when the grant was
awarded to a US company, equipment was often
purchased from China.

19. A proposed $450 million wind farm in Texas,
to be operated by Chinese using Chinese equipment, was allegedly backed by Senate Majority
Leader Harry Reid (D-Nevada) despite controversy over the source of the equipment.[89] Reid,
however, was more immediately concerned with
funding for Nevada Geothermal[90] and NRG

Energy. This last company not only received $3.8 billion in 1705 loans (nearly a fourth of the money); subsidiaries also received 39 stimulus grants.[91] Companies like this were also eligible for, and sometimes applied for, assistance from other federal departments and/or the Export-Import Bank.

20. A Canadian company, St. Clair Solar, won loans totaling $192.9 million from the Export-Import Bank in order to buy solar panels from First Solar. Since St. Clair was owned by First Solar, it was actually being assisted to buy from itself.[92]

21. In all, an estimated one quarter of the green energy stimulus dollars went to foreign-owned companies. This contrasts with President Obama's stated justification for the program: "I'm not going to . . . cede our position to China or Germany . . . who [sic] are making massive investments in clean energy technology. . . ."[93]

22. The Congressional Research Service concluded that the green energy grants had created 8,000 jobs, although some temporary, at an average cost of $1.2 million each.[94]

23. How did these companies qualify for assistance? It appears that their primary qualification was that they made campaign contributions and hired lobbyists who also made campaign contributions. But

sometimes the relationships went deeper. A small California green building supply company, Serious Materials, got stimulus money. It also got personal endorsements from President Obama and Vice President Biden. The vice president visited the company and proclaimed that it made "the most energy efficient windows in the world."

How did this happen? The company's executives had indeed made political contributions to the Democrats. But, interestingly, a vice president of the company is married to Cathy Zoi, who gave out grants from the Obama Energy Department. Disclosure documents reveal that she and her husband held stock options on 120,000 shares of the company stock.

When Ms. Zoi left Energy, she went to work for George Soros, one of the Obama administration's and Democratic Party's largest campaign donors. Soros was opening a new fund to invest in—what else?—green energy. Would some of the investments also be backed by the government employee who had succeeded Ms. Zoi? We do not know yet.[95]

24. *Washington Post* reporter Carol Leonnig noted that $2.5 billion in loans, grants, and tax breaks went to fourteen green-tech firms in which former US vice president and green tech advocate Al Gore invested. She also noted that his net worth

increased from $2 million when left office to an estimated $150 million in 2012.[96]

25. By late 2011, there were already over 100 criminal probes of green energy stimulus awards.[97] A year later, this number increased to 1,900.[98] One of the companies investigated, Abound Solar, closed its doors in the summer of 2012, leaving in its wake charges of securities fraud, consumer fraud, and financial misrepresentation. President Obama praised the company in a weekly radio address in 2009. The chief executive of the company was also invited to the White House. Despite this, when President Obama was re-elected president, *New York Times* columnist David Brooks praised the administration for its "high integrity" and "very clean" record.[99]

26. Green energy investments were accompanied by green energy training programs run by the Department of Labor. The Department's own Inspector General in 2012 found that only 16% of trainees kept the jobs they gained for more than six months. Congressman and House Oversight Committee Chairman Darrell Issa (R-California) called this program an administration "slush fund" to reward political allies "like the National Council of LaRaza, the Blue Green Alliance, and the US Steelworker's Union."[100]

27. As the green energy investments of the stimulus
    program unraveled, some of the action seemed
    to be moving to the Small Business Administra-
    tion (SBA). By the summer of 2012, the Obama
    administration's SBA was launching two new funds
    to finance start-up and new companies that are
    located in high unemployment areas or oper-
    ate in education or—yes—clean energy fields.
    These new initiatives were being undertaken even
    though the SBA was budgeting $24 billion in
    losses from its last foray into venture capital, the
    Participating Securities Program, which had been
    shut down by President George W. Bush in 2004
    after making disastrous investments under Presi-
    dent Clinton.[101]

6

Honey Pots 2:
Hurricane Sandy Relief
and the "Fiscal Cliff"

Sandy

PRESIDENT OBAMA REQUESTED $60 billion
for "emergency" relief after Hurricane Sandy
hit New Jersey and New York just before the
presidential election of November 2012. Of this total,
$36 billion was estimated to involve expenditures
that had little or nothing to do with the hurricane,
including global warming studies, additional subsidies for Amtrak, Legal Services Corp funding, even
money for fisheries as far away as American Samoa.

When Senate Majority leader Harry Reid decided he did not have the votes to overcome a filibuster in the Senate, he began to extend the bill to cover other states not affected by Sandy in hopes of securing at least seven more votes from Republican senators. For example, $100 million in housing funds was expanded to $500 million and eligibility extended to include any disaster area declared in 2011 or 2012. This made a great many states eligible, because over the two-year period the government had declared 353 disasters. This was far more than any previous two-year period, which seems to have reflected an intentional decision to broaden the definition of disaster in order to increase the president's leverage with Congress. In all, 64% of the Sandy money requested would not be spent until fiscal year 2015, in what was supposed to be emergency relief legislation.[102]

It was also notable that the Sandy bill did nothing to address the out-of-control federal flood insurance program that was already, even before Sandy, $19 billion in the red. This flood insurance encourages people to build where common sense says they should not, on beaches. Most of these structures are second homes built by affluent people, but we subsidize them with taxpayer money and money borrowed from China.[103]

"Fiscal Cliff"

President Obama and the Republicans made a deal in 2010 extending the George W. Bush tax cuts until December 31, 2012, right after the presidential election. This suited both parties: it extended the cuts, which suited the Republicans. And it enabled President Obama to run on a platform of raising taxes on the rich.

The chief argument voiced by Republicans in favor of keeping the full Bush tax cuts, including those in upper tax brackets, was that raising taxes on the "rich" would actually raise taxes on small businesses. This was correct. Most small businesses are not incorporated and instead pay taxes through the owners' 1099 personal tax forms. President Obama's response was that his proposed tax increases would only affect 3% of small businesses, but this calculation was misleading. The small businesses that would be affected actually earned 91% of small business income and also employed 54% of the entire private US workforce.[104]

Another argument the Republicans did not raise, but perhaps should have, is that higher income taxes generally hit hardest newer businesses owned by people on the rise, not established businesses owned by the old rich. This is because newer and faster-growing businesses rely most heavily on current income to finance the expansion of their businesses. They also tend to have less credit with banks and greater need for expansion capital. Businesses in this category, when taxed more, have no choice but to slow their growth, including the hiring of new employees. Economist Art Laffer has been a particularly vocal critic of higher taxes on small businesses: "Higher marginal tax rates prevent poor people from becoming rich. The only way they can get rich is by earning income, which is taxable. Once you become rich, you have ways around it."[105]

The scheduled expiration of all the Bush tax cuts, on rich and non-rich alike, was called the "fiscal cliff," a term coined by Fed Chairman Ben Bernanke. The idea was that if the all the tax cuts were rescinded, spending in the economy would fall off a cliff and the economy would be damaged. This was standard Keynesian economic doctrine, supported neither by logic nor empirical evidence, but treated by most Washington officials and politicians as beyond dispute.

The Republicans and President Obama engaged in high drama negotiations that resulted in the extension of the Bush tax cuts for all but those making $400,000 or more, a figure somewhat higher than the cut-off initially favored by President Obama, along with fewer deductions for those making $250,000. But what was really striking about the bill that passed late at night in both houses of Congress was not the treatment of the Bush tax cuts. It was the inclusion, in the bill, of a whole raft of special tax favors for industry.

Goldman Sachs, General Electric, and Citigroup got extension of a provision that allows US companies to move overseas profits into offshore financial subsidiaries, even though President Obama had criticized companies for doing just this. This one provision allowed General Electric, a key Obama ally, to avoid paying much US income tax. Some of the other 50 corporate tax breaks benefited the movie industry, another key Obama ally, green energy companies, biotechnology companies, a NASCAR racecar track owned by an ally of a Democratic senator in Michigan, and StarKist Tuna, which is close to Nancy Pelosi (D-California), former speaker of the House of Representatives.[106]

Moreover, this was not a list of corporate tax breaks sponsored by Republicans, generally thought to be closer to industry, or developed by both parties. It was a bill coming out of a Senate committee chaired by Max Baucus (D-Montana) in August 2012 and passed by the Democratic-controlled Senate, which was then blocked by the Republican-controlled House. Most Capitol Hill observers thought it was dead. President Obama, however, insisted that it be folded into the fiscal cliff bill where he knew Republicans would not be able to block it.[107]

This was President Obama's personal list of corporate tax breaks. The breaks, taken together, cost the

US government per year more than the expected tax receipts from eliminating the Bush tax cuts for those making more than $400,000 a year, $67 billion in 2013 versus $62 billion. The only difference was that the corporate tax breaks were mostly for a year to two so that the special interests involved would have to come back to get them renewed, which would in turn create plenty of incentive to make campaign contributions.

Immediately after passage of the bill that included all his own corporate tax breaks, and that wiped out any deficit reduction from his much vaunted new taxes on the rich, President Obama called for "further reforms to our tax code so that the wealthiest corporations and individuals can't take advantage of loopholes and deductions that aren't available to most taxpayers."[108]This must stand out as one of the more hypocritical statements ever made by an American president.

7

Getting Rich (or Living Rich) from Public Office

CRONYISM HAS BEEN present in American politics from the start. The first act of Congress was to pass a tariff raising revenue but also favoring manufacturing interests. Colleagues, friends, and congressional allies of the first Treasury secretary, Alexander Hamilton, used insider information to earn profits for themselves. An assistant, Alexander Duer, took bribes in exchange for tips.[109] President Jackson closed the Second Bank of the United States (the Federal Reserve of its day) in a brave effort to control its corruption of Congress. After the Civil War, government took a larger role in the economy, and both cronism and corruption sharply increased.

The emergence of government regulatory agencies before World War I opened up large new opportunities for exploitation by special interests. Ostensibly intended to prevent monopoly and other predatory pricing behavior, they could instead be used to foster and protect monopoly, as J. P. Morgan noted in a letter to business associates. He was particularly interested in controlling railroad regulation, and largely succeeded.

In 1892, US Attorney General Richard Olney explained to a former boss, a railway tycoon, how "regulatory capture" worked:

> The [Interstate Commerce] Commission (ICC) . . . is, or can be made, of great use to the railroads. It satisfies the popular clamor for a government supervision of the railroads, at the same time that supervision is almost entirely nominal. Further, the older such a commission gets to be, the more inclined it will be found to take the business and railroad view of things. . . . The part of wisdom is not to destroy the Commission, but to utilize it. [110]

In the early years of World War II, another regulatory agency, the Federal Communications Commission, which is charged with oversight of radio and television signals, had a political problem. Powerful

Georgia Congressman Eugene Cox had been paid by a private party to win FCC approval of a lucrative business transaction. Cox was not happy with his treatment by the agency, so he decided to launch a congressional investigation into its operations. FCC official Red James decided to "fix" the Cox problem by arranging the sale of radio station KTBC in Austin to Texas Congressman Lyndon Johnson's wife at a cheap price: $17,500. James knew that Johnson was personally close to House Speaker Sam Rayburn, who had the power to shut down Cox, but was reluctant to do so. KTBC's owners had petitioned the agency to allow a sale three years earlier, but were initially put on hold and then told they would sell to Mrs. Johnson.

Shortly after the sale, Mrs. Johnson requested and was granted permission by the agency to expand broadcast hours from daylight to 24 hours, move to a better AM frequency, and expand into television, which was a protected local monopoly. She was even allowed to run shows from all three major television networks, a privilege denied most other stations in the US. As a direct result, the Johnsons, who themselves had no capital the year of the sale, 1943, had become very wealthy by the time they reached the White House in 1963.

Although the station was the principal source of the president's wealth, there were rumors of other "deals" and even bribes that may have been additional sources of gain.[111] Internal Revenue Service files indicate that

LBJ and his corporate ally and benefactor, Brown and Root Company, were investigated by the agency, and almost indicted for tax evasion, but President Roosevelt, a mentor of Johnson's, quashed it. LBJ's right-hand man, Bobby Baker, was eventually sent to prison for bribery, but by then his boss was president and too powerful for government prosecutors to target.

The Johnson story has been painstakingly put together by his biographers. Most such dealings remain invisible, because powerful people want them to remain that way. Even so, there are whispers and questions.

Consider US Senate Majority Leader Harry Reid, (D-Nevada). He has gotten steadily richer from land deals back home while ostensibly working full time in Washington. How has he done this? Why is so little known about it? Why does the press not look into it?

Or consider Valerie Jarrett, president Obama's long-time friend and closest advisor in the White House. A little more is known about her wealth, also gained while holding a powerful political position. Jarrett lists on her disclosure forms an 11% stake in a Chicago luxury apartment building developed by Habitat, a private company whose name perhaps not coincidentally sounds like the completely unrelated charity Habitat for Humanity. Jarrett had been associated with the company while working as a close aide to the mayor of Chicago, Richard Daley. The company rewarded her with the stake, valued at $250,001 in 2010, but $1-5 million two years later.

Chicago city records say that the building is worth $27.2 million. But since 2008 (the year President Obama won the White House with Ms. Jarrett by his side), it has been classed as a "special commercial structure," which reduces its tax valuation by three-fourths to $6.8 million. Questions surrounding this building include: What exactly did Ms. Jarrett do to earn her stake other than give the developer access to the mayor's office? And why has the building received special tax status?[112]

Nancy Pelosi, Democrat from San Francisco and speaker of the US House 2006–2010, poses similar questions. She and her husband have grown very wealthy during her years in government. Is there a connection? Mr. Pelosi denies it: "My business dealings have nothing to do with my wife's political career."[113] Stories have circulated for years suggesting otherwise.

One persistent rumor is that campaign donors, themselves rich investors and venture capitalists, have given the Pelosis insider slices of venture deals or initial public offerings of hot stocks. That remains undocumented, but one real estate investment is known, because Mrs. Pelosi finally disclosed it publicly after years of omitting it from her public disclosure forms.

Sometime around 1999, a developer friend of the Pelosis named Tsakopoulos, one of the largest land developers in Northern California, bought undeveloped property called the Russell Ranch near Sacramento. He offered Mr. Pelosi a share. Mr. Pelosi made the investment through an S-corporation under his control which, unlike partnerships and similar forms of indirect business ownership, is not subject to federal disclosure requirements. This loophole may have been intentionally designed by House members, or may simply have been an oversight that the Pelosis and perhaps others have exploited.

Mr. Pelosi was a passive investor, that is, he left the management entirely to others. This being the case, why did Mr. Tsakopoulos want to share the opportunity with the Pelosis? No one looking from the outside can be sure. But it is known that Mr. Tsakopoulos hoped to persuade Folsom, CA to annex the property, thereby sharply increasing its value. When he succeeded in doing so, the investment's value increased by five times. Did Mr. Pelosi help? Or did having the Pelosis involved help? Again, one can only guess.

The reason this investment became public knowledge is that the Pelosis finally decided to put it on their disclosure forms, although, being made through an S-Corp, they were not technically required to do so. Why did they decide to take this step in 2010, after years of not disclosing it? The reason appears to be that the *Washington Times* began to probe business dealings between Mr. Tsakopoulos and the Pelosis following Mrs. Pelosi's public support for the nomination of Tsakapoulos's daughter, Eleni Tsakapoulos-Kounalakis, to be US ambassador to Hungary under the Obama Administration. Mrs. Pelosi called charges that she had previously hidden the business relationship "ridiculous and false," despite the earlier reported nondisclosure.

Despite Mrs. Pelosi's considerable wealth, she has also been criticized for personal use of government resources. As Speaker of the House, she reportedly reserved a Defense Department jet to take her home to San Francisco nearly every weekend, and in 2007 reportedly told the Pentagon that she wanted a plane that did not have to stop for refueling, a violation of rules. Such rides are supposed to be provided only when the plane is traveling anyway, but this is widely disregarded, notably by Mrs. Pelosi, who of course has a large say in the Defense Department budget.

In 2009, the Pentagon requested funds to buy an elite Gulfstream jet specifically to service transportation requests from Congress. The House Appropriations Committee decided one luxury plane was not enough and provided $132 million for two more similar aircraft. This was, of course, right after the Crash of 2008 when millions were losing their jobs and most people outside government were tightening their belts.[114]

Judicial Watch obtained documents under The Freedom of Information Act listing items Speaker

Pelosi's office told the Defense Department to stock in the plane that would be ferrying her back and forth between coasts. Some of these included:

> Maker's Mark whiskey, Courvoisier cognac, Johnny Walker Red scotch, Grey Goose vodka, E&J brandy, Bailey's Irish Crème, Bacardi Light rum, Jim Beam whiskey, Beefeater gin, Dewar's scotch, Bombay Sapphire gin, Jack Daniels whiskey . . . and Corona beer.

Such a list strongly suggests that the Speaker was inviting friends for an on-board party. Over two years, 2008–2009, Pelosi's trips cost taxpayers over $2 million, and the food and liquor alone cost $101,000, or almost $1,000 a week.[115]

Pelosi's trips were of course not solely back and forth to San Francisco. She was a celebrated junketer at government expense, traveling around the world. In December 2009, she flew to Copenhagen for the Global Climate Change meetings, even though these concerned a potential treaty, and treaties do not come to the House for approval, only to the Senate.[116]

Nancy Pelosi was of course not alone in the high living at government expense. On August 28, 2009, Pelosi's colleague House Majority Leader Steny H. Hoyer (D-Maryland) threw a party at historic Middleton Hall to celebrate "Women's Equality Day." The meal featured chicken cordon bleu for about 200 guests, and the expense, $5,380, was charged to the government.[117] Vice President Joe Biden ran up charges of $459,000 for himself and his entourage in London shortly after the presidential election of 2012. This came to $500 a room on average. Putting him up for one night in Paris on the same trip cost $585,000.[118]

Nor is living well limited to elected officials. Sit-ins organized by the "Occupy Wall Street" movement were aimed at the top 1% of US earners. But the demonstrators had not done their homework thoroughly. They should have known that 43% of the top 1% can be found, not on Wall Street, but in the fourteen counties surrounding Washington, DC.[119]

Elected officials do have perks not available to other government employees. Until recently, service in the US House or Senate meant that, in addition to making helpful business or investment contacts, which could lead to "sweetheart" investments or loans, one could also buy or sell stocks based on "inside information" picked up in government service.

Most people would ask: what about "insider trading" laws designed to prevent this? But Congress exempts itself from many inconvenient laws, including until recently insider trading laws. Finally a book by Peer Schweizer, *Throw Them All Out*, got enough media attention that national legislators reconsidered and decided to pass the Stock Act, putting some limits on their own gain from insider knowledge.

Legislators becoming rich, or living rich, at the public expense may not seem to affect the federal budget or the economy very much. Some of the shenanigans do have a market impact. The Johnson monopoly in Austin television no doubt raised local advertising prices. The success in winning city annexation of land held in part by the Pelosis raised the price of the land considerably. But that is not the primary point here.

The primary point is that a thriving society and economy depends on honest exchanges, and honest exchanges depend in turn on an honest government. Corruption is one of the great human impoverishers. And corruption is growing, not receding, in the United States and other developed countries as a culture of cronyism insidiously spreads, invading public, private, and nonprofit sectors, and linking them together into a network of rotten deals.

8

The Revolving Door

COLUMNIST FAREED ZAKARIA wrote in *Newsweek* that "the revolving door between Washington government offices and lobbying firms is so lucrative and so established that anyone pointing out that it is—at base—institutionalized corruption is seen as baying at the moon."[120] Presidential candidate Barack Obama promised that "when I'm president, [lobbyists] won't find a job in my White House."[121] On his first day in office, he signed an executive order forbidding employment of registered lobbyists within his administration for two years after they left their lobbying positions.

Only a few weeks later, the new president signed waivers exempting three new hires: a Deputy Secretary of Defense, a Deputy Secretary of Health and Human Services, and a Chief of Staff of the Treasury Department.[122] More and more waivers followed, 40 within a year and a half.[123] Other waivers allowed these and other appointees to involve themselves directly in matters pertaining to former clients.

In addition, the new rules applied only to registered lobbyists, thereby excluding most lawyers. It was within the rules for the administration to appoint William B. Schultz as general counsel of Health and Human Services, even though he had specialized in representing medical and drug companies regulated by the agency, and was described as a "veteran lobbying presence."[124] "Senior advisors" and of course ex-lobbyists were also not covered. Thus Vice President Biden could hire senior counselor Steve Ricchetti because he was no longer a registered lobbyist, only president of a lobbying firm![125]

Nor did existing conflict of interest rules apply to "consultants." For example, the administration decided that a Harvard professor, Ashton Carter, who became the chief weapons buyer in the Defense Department, had to recuse himself from any matter pertaining to Harvard. But he was free to involve himself in matters involving former consulting clients, including major defense contractors and Goldman Sachs.[126]

Sometimes the federal/private special interest revolving door spins so fast that it becomes almost a blur. Stacia Hylton left her job as acting deputy director of the US Marshall's Service in February 2010. She immediately garnered a large consulting contract with a private correctional company, GEO Group Inc., which had previously received a contract from Hylton's agency. Only seven months later, Hylton was nominated to return to the Marshall's Service as its head.[127]

Shortly after leaving office, Michael Chertoff, former head of the Homeland Security Department, which included the Transportation Safety Administration (TSA), began media appearances promoting "backscatter" body scanners in US airports that relied on radiation. The machines were controversial; some scientists thought the radiation could promote cancer. When a decision was made to rush the machines into airports, no one mentioned that TSA had never done any independent testing of them, but rather relied solely on the manufacturer's word.[128] Nor were many people aware that Chertoff was not simply endorsing and promoting the machines out of private conviction. He had become a paid spokesman for the scanner manufacturer.

The sums involved in these transactions can be quite large. Nancy-Ann DeParle was head of what is now the Centers for Medicare and Medicaid Services under President Clinton, and was brought back into government by President Obama to be his White

House Director of the Office of Health Reform, from which she orchestrated the healthcare "reform" bill. While out of government for eight years, she earned $6.6 million in corporate director's fees, $2.3 million during 2008 and the first half of 2009 alone. Companies that asked her to join their boards had government relations problems they clearly hoped she could help solve, including criminal investigations related to Medicare billing and pleading guilty to felony charges.[129]

Ms. DeParle was not the only White House or Hill staffer working on the healthcare bill who had prior corporate relationships. On Capitol Hill, the legislation was shaped in the Senate by the Health, Education, Labor and Pension Committee, and the Finance Committee. Here is a list of the Finance Committee staff members with previous corporate ties published by *Politico*:

- Before she was hired last year as senior counsel to Finance Committee Chairman Max Caucus (D-Montana), Liz Fowler worked as a highly paid public policy advisor for WellPoint Inc., the nation's largest publicly traded health benefits company.

- Mark Hayes, health policy director and chief health counsel for Finance Committee ranking member Chuck Grassley (R-Iowa), is married to a registered lobbyist for a firm that represents drug companies and hospital groups. . . .

- Frederick Isasi, a health policy adviser to Senator Jeff Bingaman (D-New Mexico), was a registered lobbyist at Powell Goldstein, where his clients included public hospitals and the American Stroke Association.

- Kate Spaziani, senior health policy aide to Senator Kent Conrad (D-North Dakota), was also a registered lobbyist at Powell Goldstein. . . . According to the group Public Accountability Initiative, which tracks politicians' ties to various interest, more than 500 former congressional aides have gone on to become healthcare lobbyists.[130]

We will have more to say about this when we discuss the healthcare industry. For example, we will recount how the head of the US Center for Disease Control, Julie Gerberding, fast-tracked a controversial and apparently dangerous vaccine which her agency had itself invented and licensed to Merck, then left the government to become head of Merck's vaccine division. When we discuss the food industry, we will see how a Monsanto lawyer and executive, Michael Taylor, joined the government twice just in time to write favorable rules about or otherwise influence the regulation of controversial and apparently dangerous Monsanto products.

In most cases, government employees who are angling for a job in a private company are discrete about it. They speak indirectly and put nothing in an email. Timothy Cannon, former director of the human capital division of the Federal Emergency Management Agency (FEMA), was an exception. He delivered a large contract to a private company, got the contract increased, and was too obvious about it, with the result that he was exposed by a whistleblower and ended up pleading guilty to a felony.[131]

The $6 million contract was for "The Best Workforce Initiative" program. What, one might ask, is the Best Workforce Initiative? What conceivable connection does it have to FEMA's mission of providing relief after natural disasters? In addition, what is FEMA's human capital division, and how does that fit the mission? What Cannon did was illegal, but it seems to represent only the most visible part of what is a larger web of waste and corruption.

Sometimes it is not even necessary for the revolving door to revolve in order for someone to make money. After Barack Obama was elected to the Senate in 2004, his wife's salary at the University of Chicago Medical Center jumped from $121,910 to $316,962, according to tax returns. The next year, Senator Obama sought to earmark $1 million for the Center, which later received a $6 million grant under President Obama's Affordable Care Act.[132] It is interesting that Mrs. Obama's position simply disappeared when she left for the White House.[133]

There is nothing unusual about this story. Several prominent senators have wives or children who work as lobbyists. These lobbyists are barred from approaching their husband's or father's office, but nevertheless have much more access to other offices because of the family connection. And when the senator retires from office, then he or she may take one of these lucrative positions.

For example, Senator Ben Nelson (D-Nebraska), on leaving the US Senate to become head of the National Association of Insurance Commissioners and also "senior partner" at a lobbying firm, said that it was "an important and exciting time in the regulatory community." He did not mention that part of the excitement was created by two new bills, Obamacare and Dodd-Frank, that he had played a critical role in passing and that would now be entering years of massive regulation writing, with hundreds of thousands of pages of regulations expected. Obamacare in particular would not have passed without his vote and had not been popular among his constituents.[134]

Under current rules, it is even possible to work in government and at the same time indirectly benefit financially from what you are doing. David Axelrod is one of President Obama's most senior White House advisors and his chief campaign strategist. Before taking on this role, he was president and sole owner of a public relations firm, AKPD Message and Media, where his son continues to work, and which owes him a $2 million buyout payable in four annual installments.

When drug companies, health insurance companies such as the American Association of Retired Persons (AARP), the American Medical Association, (AMA), and unions (such as the powerful Service Employees International Union) collectively pledged to spend hundreds of millions on ads supporting the Obama health reform act, what agency did they choose for $24 million of this money? None other than AKPD, which also employed former Obama campaign director David Plouffe. Did another of Mr. Axelrod's former companies, ASK Public Strategies (which owed its founder another $1 million) also benefit from this advertising campaign? We do not know. ASK will not say.[135] David Plouffe also got in the news by accepting a $100,000 speaking fee from a South African company with close ties to Iran. Did Mr Plouffe really think they were paying him that much just to hear him speak?[136]

Part 3

Crony Finance

9

"Government Sachs": Revolving Door Prodigy and Power Behind the Throne

2012 GOP PRESIDENTIAL candidate Herman Cain held that "Protesting Wall Street and the bankers is basically saying you are anti-capitalist."[137] This was complete nonsense. Perhaps Cain was hoping for Wall Street campaign contributions. As a businessman, he should have known that Wall Street is not the center of market capitalism. It is just the opposite: the center of government-sponsored enterprise.

This is a game managed from Washington, with often bewilderingly complex, indeed unfathomable rules, just the place to enrich crony capitalists and fill political campaign coffers.

At the center of Wall Street stands Goldman Sachs, master of the crony influence game. As US Representative Peter DeFazio (D-Oregon) says, "They've been wired through the Clinton years, the Bush years, and before that, they have a lot of heavy hitters." This is certainly confirmed by the record.[138]

Here are some influential people using the revolving door between Goldman Sachs and government:

Europe

GOLDMAN SACHS	GOVERNMENT
Antonio Borges, vice chair, GS International	Head of European Department of International Monetary Fund
Ben Broadbent, economist	Bank of England
Mark Carney, managing director	Governor, Bank of Canada, now governor Bank of England
Petros Christadoulou	Head of Greek Debt Management Agency
Gavin Davies, chief economist	Chair, BBC
Mario Draghi, vice chair GS International	Head of Bank of Italy, now head of European Central Bank
Lord Brian Griffith, international advisor	Aide to UK prime minister
Otmar Issing, advisor	Board member European Central Bank, helped create euro

Europe (cont'd.)

GOLDMAN SACHS	GOVERNMENT
Karel van Miert, international advisor	European community commissioner
Mario Monti, international advisor	Italian prime minister
Romano Prodi, international advisor	Twice Italian prime minister
Peter Sutherland, non-exec. director, GS International	Attorney general of Ireland
Sushil Wadhwani, director Equity Strategy	Bank of England
David Walton, economist (1963–2006)	Bank of England

Obama Administration

GOLDMAN SACHS	GOVERNMENT
Gregory Craig, lawyer for Goldman	White House chief counsel
Thomas Donilon, outside lawyer	Deputy national security advisor
Rahm Emanuel, consultant[139]	White House chief of staff
Dina Farrell, financial analyst	National Economic Council
Gary Gensler, co-head finance worldwide	Chairman of US Commodity Futures Commission, undersecretary of Treasury under Clinton
Robert D. Hormats, vice chair international	Undersecretary of State
Alexander Lasry, lobbying	White House special assistant
Philip Murphy, senior director	US ambassador to Germany

Obama Administration (cont'd.)

GOLDMAN SACHS	GOVERNMENT
Mark Patterson, lobbyist	Treasury chief of staff
Gene Sperling, consultant (Paid $888,000 to advise on charitable giving, a very unusual fee for such work. Thought by some to be so high for commercial, not charitable reasons, which could be illegal if paid through a foundation.[140] Shortly thereafter Sperling joined the Obama Administration's Treasury Department to oversee the Wall Street bail-out.)	Chief economic advisor, had also served Clinton Administration Treasury Department
Adam Storch, VP	Chief operating officer of SEC Enforcement Division (during period in which SEC investigated Goldman Sachs)
Larry Summers, consultant (a single speech at the firm earned a fee of $135,000)[141]	Chief economic advisor

George W. Bush Administration

GOLDMAN SACHS	GOVERNMENT
Joshua Bolten, lawyer and lobbyist	White House chief of staff, budget director
Edward C. Forst, head investment management	Advisor to Treasury Secretary Paulson, 2008
Randall M. Fort, director, global security	Assistant secretary of State
Stephen Friedman, former co-chairman and CEO	Director, National Economic Council, chairman New York Fed

George W. Bush Administration (cont'd.)

GOLDMAN SACHS	GOVERNMENT
Reuben Jeffery, III, managing partner, Paris	Undersecretary of State
Neal Kashkari, VP	Various Treasury posts including responsibility for TARP (Troubled Asset Relief Program)
Dan Jester, VP, advisor to Treasury Secretary Paulson	Major campaign fundraiser for Bush
Todd Malan, lobbyist	US Trade Representative's Office
Henry "Hank" Paulson (former Goldman CEO)	Secretary of the Treasury during Crash of 2008. Rescued Goldman Sachs from probable bankruptcy. Earlier service under Nixon.
Steve Shafran, trader	Advisor to Treasury Secretary Paulson
Faryar Shirzad, global lobbyist	National Security Council, Commerce Department
Robert K. Steel, vice chair	Undersecretary Treasury during Crash of 2008
Kendrick Wilson, Sr., investment banker	Advisor to Treasury Secretary Paulson
Robert Zoellick, vice chair international	President, World Bank

Clinton Administration

GOLDMAN SACHS	GOVERNMENT
Kenneth D. Brody, member management committee	Head of Export-Import Bank
Arthur Levitt, advisor	Chairman, Securities and Exchange Commission (SEC)

Clinton Administration (cont'd.)

GOLDMAN SACHS	GOVERNMENT
Robert Rubin, co-CEO	Secretary of Treasury (where he mentored both Larry Summers and Tim Geithner, future Treasury secretaries)
Sonal Shah, VP, economist	Treasury Department, various posts, also Obama-Biden transition
Richard Y. Roberts, outside lobbyist	SEC commissioner
Marti Thomas, lobbyist	Treasury Department, former top House aide

Other

GOLDMAN SACHS	GOVERNMENT
Bernard W. Aronson, international advisor	Carter White House, G. H. W. Bush State Department
Kathleen Brown, senior advisor	California State treasurer
Robert Cogorno, outside lobbyist	Top House aide
Kenneth Connolly, VP, lobbyist	Top Senate aide
E. Gerald Corrigan, chair holding company	President, New York Fed
Jon Corzine, former CEO	US Senator, Governor of New Jersey
Kenneth Duberstein, outside lobbyist	Reagan chief of staff
William Dudley, managing director	President, New York Fed
Steven Elmendorf, outside lobbyist	Top House aide
Harold Ford, Sr., outside lobbyist	US congressman

Other (cont'd.)

GOLDMAN SACHS	GOVERNMENT
Judd Gregg, consultant	Senator
Henry H. Fowler, partner	Secretary of Treasury under Johnson
Jim Hines, VP	US congressman
Chris Javens, lobbyist	Top Senate aide
Richard Gephardt, outside lobbyist	US congressman in House Democratic leadership and presidential candidate
Lori E. Laudien, lobbyist	Top Senate aide
Michael Paese, director, Goldman Sachs lobbying	Top House aide to Financial Services Committee Chairman Barney Frank
Richard Y. Roberts, managing director	SEC commissioner
Paul Sarbanes, outside firm lobbyist	US Senator, author of Sarbanes-Oxley Financial Oversight legislation
Eric Veland, lobbyist	Chief of staff for former Senate Majority leader Bill Frist (R-Tennessee)
John C. Whitehead (co-chair Goldman Sachs)	Deputy secretary of State under Reagan and chair of New York Fed

Goldman Sachs gains immense political clout from this web of government connections. But the money it spends on lobbying, and the campaign funds it donates or raises, also contribute to its power. Its federal lobbying expenditure reached $4.6 million in 2010,[142] the year the SEC charged the firm with civil fraud. Federal political donations rose to $290,500[143] the month just prior to the announcement, when everyone already suspected what was coming, and for the two election cycles 2006–2008 and 2008–2010, and partial cycle 2010–8/2012 totaled $14.4 million.[144] This made Goldman Sachs by far the biggest lobbying force and campaign contributor among financial firms.

What Goldman Sachs got in return:

1. Survival

Lehman Brothers, a chief rival of Goldman Sachs, collapsed in the fall of 2008. Its request to convert to a deposit-taking bank, which would have placed it under the protection of the federal government and given it access to limitless government cash, was denied by the Federal Reserve and Treasury Departments. Very shortly after Lehman's bankruptcy, Goldman Sachs and Morgan Stanley were granted this same privilege.

Conversion to bank status immediately told the world that Goldman Sachs and Morgan Stanley would not be allowed to fail. But that was only the beginning. The two firms also received Troubled Asset Relief Program (TARP) funds, $10 billion to Goldman Sachs. They profited from a secret New York Fed loan at 0.01%, $30 billion to Goldman Sachs. They benefited from FDIC and other guarantees for their outside borrowing, $43.5 billion to Goldman Sachs. They were given access to the Fed's general borrowing window for banks, which provided access to newly printed money at minimal rates (lower than market and even lower than inflation), a privilege that continues to this day. By moving more and more of their derivatives business to the new bank subsidiary, they could get implicit government insurance for that as well.

All of these maneuvers were only possible in the first place because former Goldman Sachs Co-CEO Robert Rubin, when secretary of the Treasury under President Clinton, led a repeal of the Glass-Steagall Act, a legislative initiative that had ensured plentiful Wall Street campaign contributions to Clinton. Glass-Steagall, passed during the Great Depression, prohibited any combination of deposit-taking banking with the kind of investment banking, trading, and speculating activities that provided most of Goldman Sachs's profits. So, in effect, one former Goldman Sachs head laid the groundwork for Goldman Sachs to become a federally protected bank, his protégé in the Treasury Department, Tim Geithner, gave consent when it was needed in 2008, and another former Goldman Sachs head, Paulson, then Treasury Secretary, facilitated and blessed the maneuver.

At the same time, the US government also bailed out AIG, an insurance company that owed money to Goldman Sachs. Most knowledgeable observers assumed that the payout on mortgage securities protection contracts would be negotiated and reduced.

But on the instruction of New York Fed President Tim Geithner, AIG paid out every penny, a total of almost $13 billion. Geithner supporters later pointed out that the US government was eventually able to sell its stock in AIG back into the stock market at a high enough price to repay the bail-out, even with the indirect payoff to Goldman Sachs. But in reality the recovery of AIG bail-out funds was only possible because the stock market had been inflated sufficiently by US Federal Reserve pumping to sell back the AIG stock without a loss.

Goldman Sachs stated publicly that the extra $13 billion it received from AIG, courtesy of Tim Geithner, was not critical, because other hedges protected against an AIG default on the obligation. It is doubtful, however, that the other hedges, if they existed, would have paid off, and certainly not dollar for dollar. As the office of the Inspector General for TARP reported, the decision by Geithner to pay full price to Goldman Sachs "effectively transferred tens of billions of dollars of cash from the Government to AIG's counterparties (such as Goldman Sachs)."[145]

It is also highly relevant that when Geithner ordered full payment by AIG to Goldman Sachs, using government funds, he knew that both Merrill Lynch and Citigroup had only a few months earlier taken large losses on their securities protection contracts with insurers. Merrill Lynch, for example, had accepted $500 million against a $3.7 billion claim on Security Capital Assurance Ltd. in late July 2008.[146]

Why then were firms devoted primarily to securities sales, trading, financial insurance, or just speculating brought under the protection of the federal government, and in the case of Goldman Sachs even allowed to pretend they were deposit-taking banks? The usual answer is that regulators considered them "too big to fail," that is, so large that their failure would be too painful for the system to absorb. This is specious reasoning. There is no shortage of banks or securities firms in the US. If the giants had failed, their valuable assets and employees would have been absorbed by other, more prudent firms, and the economy would have gone on, stronger, not weaker, for the purging of unsuccessful speculators and rotten assets.

Even if one accepts the phony "too big to fail" rationale, why were Goldman Sachs and Morgan Stanley saved when Lehman was abandoned? The most likely answer is that the secretary of the Treasury, Hank Paulson, at that moment had arrived from Goldman Sachs, where he had been CEO and also a major campaign fundraiser for President Bush. He and Fed President Geithner agreed that Goldman Sachs had to be saved.

Luckily for Morgan Stanley, both Paulson and everyone around him knew that they could not rescue Goldman Sachs alone among the then-non-banking financial behemoths. It is a reasonable conjecture that Morgan Stanley got a free ride, mostly to provide cover for the Goldman Sachs rescue, especially after some Japanese investors provided additional outside capital.

As the crisis unfolded, Hank Paulson was initially constrained by federal ethics rules from speaking to the firm where he had spent his career or participating in decisions that affected it. But that was soon finessed. As *New York Times* reporter Andrew Ross Sorkin explained, "[Paulson] had enough of recusing himself. . . . [He] appreciated that the 'optics' of a waiver to engage with his former employer were problematic, but he hoped it would remain a secret. . . ."[147]

The White House was consulted and in short order the Treasury ethics office granted the waiver based on an "overwhelming public interest." Over the next few days, Paulson spoke to the CEO of Goldman Sachs, Lloyd Blankfein, over twenty times. He also brought in a group of Goldman executives to help manage the crisis. In a sense, management was "outsourced" to the firm that had the most to gain from what the government was doing. As a *New York Magazine* article noted, "The firm nearly went under even after the AIG bail-out." Interestingly, when Tim Geithner came in as Treasury secretary under President Obama, the constant telephone contact between the Treasury secretary and the Goldman Sachs CEO continued unabated, with conversations almost every other day according to logs obtained under the Freedom of Information Act.

2. Legal Protection

Goldman Sachs also needed and got legal protection. During 2006 and 2007, it sold $40 billion of securities backed by poor quality home mortgages. By early 2007, it was buying securities that would make money if the mortgage securities tanked, including the contracts with AIG, but without telling the buyers of the mortgages.

Some of this is even on the record. An Australian fund, Basis Capital, bought $100 million of subprime mortgage securities from Goldman Sachs on June 2007, partly with borrowed money, after being told to expect a 60% return. A Goldman Sachs salesman sent an email describing the buyer as a "white elephant, flying pig and unicorn all at once," by which he presumably meant he could not believe his luck in finding anyone so gullible. Only 16 days after the sale, Goldman Sachs was demanding more money from Basis to support the loan. Within a month, Basis had lost $37.5 million and was forced to file for bankruptcy.[148]

Professor Laurence Kotlikoff, a financial expert from Boston University, has said that

> the Securities and Exchange Commission
> should be very interested in any financial
> company that secretly decides a financial

product is a loser and then goes out and
actively markets that product or very similar products to unsuspecting customers
without disclosing its true opinion. This
is fraud and should be prosecuted.

But the SEC did not prosecute. It did not seem interested in any of this.

Was this in any way related to a Goldman Sachs
vice president, Adam Storch, becoming the managing executive of the SEC's enforcement division on
October 16, 2009?[149] Or was the problem broader,
as described by investigative reporter Matt Taibi of
Rolling Stone:

Criminal justice, as it pertains to the Gold-
mans and Morgan Stanleys of the world, is
not adversarial combat, with cops and crooks
duking it out in interrogating rooms and
courthouses. Instead, it's a cocktail party
between friends and colleagues who from
month to month and year to year are con-
stantly switching sides and trading hats.[150]

No wonder a Goldman Sachs lobbyist was quoted
by *Politico* saying in April 2010: "We are not against
regulation. We're for regulation. We partner with
regulators."[151]

The SEC did file a civil fraud complaint against
Goldman Sachs in April 2010, charging that it had

"rented" its name in 2007 to a fund operator who had bilked investors of $1 billion. During the period over which Goldman Sachs lawyers negotiated with SEC staff over this "Abacus" case, Goldman Sachs CEO Lloyd Blankfein visited the White House twice as an honored guest of President Obama. The fine of $550 million paid by Goldman Sachs three months later (without admitting guilt) represented only 4% of Goldman Sachs profits in 2007 and a tiny fraction of all the bail-out aid received earlier.

The SEC did not turn over its files to the Justice Department for prosecution, as it is legally required to do if it believes a crime has been committed. Nor did the Justice Department choose to investigate on its own. Even when the chairman of a Senate Committee, Carl Levin (D-Michigan), submitted a 650-page report to Justice stating that Goldman Sachs executives, including the CEO, had "clearly misled their clients and . . . misled the Congress [under oath in hearings]," the Department chose to sit on its hands and not investigate.[152]

What was going on here? During the Savings and Loan crisis of the 1980s, federal prosecutors filed over a thousand cases and won 90% of them.[153] After the Crash, the Justice Department vigorously pursued fraud and other charges against small-time financial operators unconnected to the big Wall Street firms.[154] Yet Wall Street remained untouched. Even when

MF Global, led by former US Senator and Governor (D-New Jersey) and former Goldman Sachs CEO Jon Corzine, announced that over $1 billion of its customers' money had gone missing,[155] there was great doubt that Justice would pursue the case.

Shortly after his election, President Obama reportedly told a group of Wall Street chief executives, gathered at the White House: "My administration is the only thing between you and the pitchforks."[156] Whose pitchforks? The Justice Department's? Was the president holding back the investigators?

Goldman Sachs had been the second largest contributor to the Obama campaign, donating almost $1 million, multiples of what it had given to his Republican opponent, John McCain. Jon Corzine had been a "bundler" who brought in $500,000 to the 2008 campaign. Vice President Biden, before Corzine's disgrace, praised him as the first person the president called for economic advice after the election.

So long as Wall Street remained unindicted, the checks would flow and, very importantly, could be cashed. Fear of indictment would mean more and more checks. Goldman Sachs contributions noticeably spiked the month before the SEC civil charge, fell right after the charges (to preserve appearances), only to ramp up again after the settlement.

Critics noted that the Justice Department was investigating the Macau casinos of Sheldon Adelson, billionaire contributor to Republicans.[157] Why Adelson but not Democratic donors? It was also noteworthy that Attorney General Eric Holder left the Clinton Justice Department to join the law firm of Covington and Burling, before returning to Justice in the top job, and that Covington and Burling represented many Wall Street firms. Perhaps, it was speculated, Holder was not just thinking about campaign contributions from Wall Street, but also about future million dollar legal fees? The circumstances, including the lack of Wall Street prosecutions after the Crash, the size of Wall Street campaign contributions, and the spinning, not just revolving, door between Wall Street and government all contributed to suspicion.

3. Profits

The millions spent by Goldman Sachs on lobbying, campaign contributions, and hiring former government employees may have staved off bankruptcy during the Crash. They may also have provided important defenses against legal challenges. But government-affiliated firms play offense as well as defense. They want to turn their government connections into profit, if possible enormous profit, and Goldman Sachs has been very successful in doing so.

Goldman Sachs is now run from a massive new headquarters building in Manhattan. By locating across from where the World Trade Center once stood, the firm was able to finance it with $1.65 billion of tax-free "Liberty Bonds." Interest savings are expected to total $175 million over 30 years. State and city provided an additional $115 million in job-grant funds, tax exemptions, and energy discounts.[158]

Government connections conferred many other benefits. With Lehman Brothers gone and other former competitors such as Merrill Lynch a shadow of their old selves, competition for securities trades decreased and "spreads" (profits) increased. In some areas of the market post-Crash, Goldman Sachs enjoyed what former employee Anthony Scaramucci called "a near monopoly."[159]

Had it passed, the Over-the-Counter Derivatives Markets Act of 2009 would have given Goldman Sachs and eight other banks government-sanctioned control over the entire derivatives market at a time when the Commodity Futures Trading Commission was led by Gary Gensler, a former Goldman senior executive. The 2010 Dodd-Frank Act did not go that far, but did seem to codify the "too big to fail" doctrine while pretending to do the opposite. Being "too big to fail" gave Goldman Sachs a significant competitive advantage when it borrowed money, whether from the Fed or from other parties. As Simon Johnson, former chief economist of the International Monetary Fund (IMF) explains:

> Everyone I've spoken to in the last year or
> so regards Goldman and other big banks
> as implicitly backed by the full faith and
> credit of the United States Treasury. This
> lowers Goldman's cost of funds, allows it
> to borrow more, and encourages ... [it] to
> become even larger.[160]

A report from Moody's, one of the leading bond rating agencies, indicated that presumed government backing of a Wall Street firm is worth "five notches." This means that a security that would have been rated Baa3 rises to A2, which produces a sizeable reduction of interest expense.[161] Moody's by the way is also a government-sponsored enterprise. Much of its revenue derives from quasi-monopoly status granted by Washington.

In light of all this, it is hardly surprising that Wall Street profits in the three years following the Crash exceeded the eight years leading up to it. By the summer of 2009, Goldman Sachs's salary and bonus pool had completely recovered from the Crash and stood at $11.36 billion (for six months). The share price, which hit an intra-day low of $47 had also recovered to $125, although still below the previous high.

Goldman CEO Lloyd Blankfein, sitting high in his Manhattan aerie, seemed uncharacteristically content by the end of 2009:

I'm charged with managing and preserving the franchise for the good of shareholders, and while I don't want to sound highfalutin, it is also for the good of America. I'm up-front about that. I think a strong Goldman Sachs is good for the country.[162]

10

"Government Electric":
Wall Street Masquerading
as Main Street

D URING THE PRESIDENTIAL campaign of
2012, an online commentator observed that
President Obama had not met with his Jobs
Council for six months. How could this be, the commentator asked, when jobs were foremost on the president's agenda? The answer was not hard to discover.

The Council was headed by General Electric CEO
Jeffrey Immelt, a noted Obama political backer. Other
members included Penny Pritzker, an heiress who
served as Obama's Finance chairwoman in 2008, and
Richard Trumpka, president of the AFL-CIO, one of

the largest Obama campaign contributors. The group was established after the 2010 mid-term election losses as a device to emphasize the administration's focus on jobs but, more importantly, to recognize political allies and campaign donors and prepare for the 2012 presidential election. This was more or less acknowledged when, after the president's re-election, it was disbanded, despite the persistence of high unemployment.

Why had the president chosen General Electric's Immelt in particular as the head of this campaign arm? For one reason, Immelt was sympathetic to the president's brand of state-led capitalism. He had gone so far as to say of China in a television interview: "The one thing that actually works, state run communism, may not be your cup of tea, but their government works."[163]

In addition, employees of General Electric as a group had been Obama's 9th largest campaign contributor in 2008, donating $529,855. These donations in part reflected the company's close and indeed symbiotic relationship with government in finance, defense, green energy, television, technology, and export, and its status as a primary beneficiary of the administration's stimulus bill. It was impossible to say where the government stopped and General Electric began and vice versa.

Even more importantly, the government rescued the company from what seemed likely to be bankruptcy in 2008–2009. It also let the company off with an exceptionally mild slap-on-the-wrist fine of $50 million for cooking its books in the late 1990s and 2000s,[164] when there might instead have been a large fine and criminal fraud charges. As a further indication of its exceptionally close ties, the Obama administration inserted language into the late 2012 fiscal cliff bill that enabled the company to avoid paying much federal income taxes.[165]

How had General Electric come to be in need of a government rescue during the Crash of 2008? For most of its history, the company was considered the bluest of blue chip firms, the last company that anybody would have expected to be in need of a rescue. Prior to the Crash of 2008, it enjoyed the highest possible score from the financial rating agencies. There was a problem, however: the rating was undeserved, perhaps the result of rating agency myopia, perhaps some behind-closed-door deal.

GE Capital, the company's finance arm, was the fastest growing part of the company. By 2007, it contributed almost 40% of revenues and almost half of profits. It generated these revenues and profits by using the company's triple A financial rating to borrow money at rates even lower than paid by banks for short periods of time and then relending for longer periods to consumers, including sub-prime borrowers. This was a classic house of cards. It should have resulted in the company's bankruptcy. But when, in September, 2008, GE ran out of credit, and the survival of the company suddenly became doubtful, Immelt knew what to do.

David Stockman, Budget Director under President Reagan and professional investor, described what happened:

> The nation's number one crony capitalist— Jeff Immelt of GE—jumped on the phone to [Treasury] Secretary Paulson and yelled "fire!" Soon the Fed and FDIC stopped the commercial-paper [short-term corporate debt] unwind dead in its track by essentially nationalizing the entire market. Even a cursory look at the data, however, shows that Immelt's SOS call was a self-serving crock.
>
> First, about $1 trillion of the $2 trillion in outstanding commercial paper was of the so-called ABCP type—paper backed by packages of consumer loans such as credit cards, auto loans, and student loans. . . .
>
> Had every single ABCP conduit been liquidated for want of commercial-paper funding—and over the past three years most have been—not a single consumer would have been denied a credit card authorization or car loan. . . .

Another $400 billion of the sector was industrial-company commercial paper—the kind of facility that some blue chip companies used to fund their payroll. But there was not a single industrial company in America then issuing commercial paper that did not also have a standby bank line. . . . Their banks had a contractual obligation to fund these backup lines, and none refused. There was never a chance that payrolls would not be met.

The last $600 billion of CP (commercial paper) is where the real crony capitalist stench lies. There were three huge users in the finance company sector—CIT, GMAC (General Motors financing arm), and GE Capital. At the time of the crisis, the latter had asset footings of $600 billion—most of it long-term, highly illiquid, and sometimes sketchy corporate and commercial real estate loans.

In violation of every rule of sound banking, more than $80 billion of these positions were funded in the super-cheap commercial paper market. This maneuver fattened spreads (revenues) on GE's loan book and produced big management bonuses, too.

But it also raised to a whole new level the ancient banking folly of mismatching short and hot liabilities with long and slow assets.

Under free market rules, an inability to roll its $80 billion in commercial paper would have forced GE Capital into a fire sale of illiquid loan assets at deep discounts, thereby incurring heavy losses and a reversal of its prior phony profits; or in the alternative, it could have held on to its loan book, and issued massively dilutive amounts of common stock or subordinated debt to close its sudden funding gap.

Either way, GE's shareholders would have taken the beating they deserved for overvaluing the company's true earnings and for putting reckless managers in charge of the store.

So the financial meltdown during those eventful weeks was not triggered by the financial equivalent of a comet from deep space—but resulted from leveraged speculation that should have been punishable by ordinary market rules.

So in the fall of 2008, the US supposedly stood on the edge of an abyss, with a likely shutdown of the entire financial system, and a Depression from which we might never emerge. But this was actually just hyperbole, a way to scare President George W. Bush and members of Congress. No wonder the former said that "I've abandoned free market principles to save the free market system." To say something so foolish in public in a television interview, he must have actually believed it.

Secretary Paulson is also alleged to have said, after receiving Immelt's desperate call in September 2008, that he realized the crisis had now spread from Wall Street to Main Street. But he must have known that GE was, by that time, the very embodiment of Wall Street, despite being headquartered nearby in Connecticut. No doubt "helping Main Street" provided good cover for, among other things, saving Paulson's Goldman Sachs.

By the time the Obama Administration arrived, GE spent more money on lobbying than any other company. Immelt was asked first to join the President's Economic Recovery Advisory Board and then, as we have noted, to chair the Council on Jobs and Competitiveness. When the administration's Environmental Protection Agency (EPA) began enforcing new rules to reduce greenhouse gas emissions, the very first exemption was granted to a GE-powered facility, the Avenal Power Center in California.[166] Meanwhile GE built a part for General Motors' electric car, the Chevy Volt, a favorite project of the administration that had been given hidden subsidies of as much as $250,000 per vehicle along with buyer tax credits.[167] When that proved insufficient to get the car sold, the government bought thousands of Volts for its own fleet.

It was potentially embarrassing to the administration that GE outsourced so many jobs overseas. For example, when Congress outlawed old-fashioned incandescent light bulbs, partly at GE's urging, manufacture of the new fluorescent bulbs was moved from GE's light bulb plants in Ohio and Kentucky to China. Also potentially embarrassing, but little known, was that the fluorescents contained mercury, an environmental hazard, and that some of the Chinese workers had reportedly been poisoned by exposure to it.[168] None of this, however, kept GE from benefiting, directly or indirectly, from what may have been billions in Stimulus Act grants.

Part 4

Crony Food

11

Monsanto's Massive Experiment with Our Health

MANY COMPANIES HOPE to send an employee into a government agency to influence regulation. How much better if the employee can actually shape government regulation to promote and sell a specific product! Monsanto seems to have accomplished this—and much more.

Michael Taylor is among a number of people with Monsanto ties who have worked in government in recent years.* He worked for the Nixon and Reagan Food and Drug Administration in the 1970s, then became a lawyer representing Monsanto. In

---

* See footnote table on the next page.

1991, he returned to the FDA as Deputy Commissioner for Policy under George H. W. Bush, and helped secure approval for Monsanto's genetically engineered bovine (cow) growth hormone, despite it being banned in Canada, Europe, Japan, Australia, and New Zealand.

This was only a start for Taylor. He also did not like some producers advertising their milk as bovine growth hormone free. That seemed to put Monsanto's product in an unfavorable light. So in 1994 he wrote a guidance document from within the FDA requiring that any food label describing the product as bovine growth hormone free must also include these words: "The FDA has determined . . . no significant difference has been shown between milk derived from [BGH] and non-[BGH] supplemented cows."

MONSANTO	US GOVERNMENT
Suzanne Sechen, worked on Monsanto funded academic research	A primary reviewer for bovine growth hormone in FDA
Linda J. Fisher, VP, lobbyist for Monsanto	Assistant Administrator at EPA
Michael Friedman, MD, Sr. VP, GD Searle, subsidiary of Monsanto	Acting Commissioner of FDA
Marcia Hale, International lobbyist, Monsanto	Assistant to President under President Clinton
Michael (Mickey) Kantor, director	Secretary of Commerce and US Trade Representative under President Clinton
William D. Ruckelshaus, director	Head of EPA under both Presidents Nixon and Reagan

It apparently did not concern Taylor that this new pronouncement by the FDA was unsupported by either Monsanto or FDA studies. A private company making any such unsupported claim could have been charged with fraud. But since it came out of the FDA, milk producers would place themselves at legal risk by not printing it on their label.

Taylor moved to the US Department of Agriculture (USDA) in the mid-1990s. During this period, he tried to persuade the FDA and Federal Trade Commission (FTC) to take a further step and make it illegal for dairies to make any claim to a bovine growth hormone free product. Failing in that, he reached out to state governments to make such a claim illegal at the state level. This was finally blocked by a court decision in Ohio that there was indeed a "compositional difference" between BGH and non-BGH-treated milk. Long before this 2010 ruling, Taylor had returned to Monsanto as a vice president, and then returned to President Obama's FDA, first as Senior Advisor on Food Safety and then Deputy Commissioner for Foods.[169]

Taylor's story, however, is not just about milk, or even mainly about milk. During his second posting at the FDA, as Deputy Commissioner for Policy 1991–1994, Agency scientists were grappling with questions about the overall safety of genetically engineered foods (often labeled Genetically Modified Organisms). As Jeffrey Smith notes,

> [Internal] memo after memo described toxins, new diseases, nutritional deficiencies, and hard to detect allergens. [Staff scientists] were adamant that the technology carried 'serious health hazards,' and required careful, long-term research, including human studies. . . .

The Agency, under Taylor's and later under others' leadership, simply ignored these findings. No human studies were required. GMO foods were allowed to enter the food supply unregulated by the FDA and barely regulated by the USDA, which views them as an important US export product. By 2012, in the US, 90% of sugar beets (representing half of overall sugar production) was GMO, 85% of soybeans (which are to be found in 70% of all supermarket food products), and 85% of corn, including the corn used to make high fructose corn syrup, a sweetener used in most soft drinks and processed foods.

The few scientists trying to conduct independent research on GMO often found their careers damaged. Most food research, conferences, and fellowships are funded by "Big Food" companies including Monsanto, which has a chilling effect. Even sympathetic colleagues may be reluctant to back those who dare speak out.

Those who persevered in conducting independent research, often abroad, reported worrisome findings.

An Austrian study found that mice fed GMO corn seemed fine in the first and second generations, but by the third were sterile. A Russian study of hamsters fed GMO soybeans found a similar result. Could human beings exhibit a similar, delayed response? No one knows. Another, unrelated study showed that the pesticide used in large quantities on engineered Roundup Ready crops is toxic to male testicle cells and threatens both testosterone synthesis and sperm count.

Reductions of testosterone, fertility problems, sterility, infant deaths, and other "reproduction" issues are not the only ones linked to GMO foods in recent animal research, the only available research in the absence of human studies. Other issues listed by the Alliance for Natural Health-USA include:

- immune system dysregulation, which changes the number of immune response cells showing up in the gut, spleen, and blood—all of which points to an allergenic and inflammatory response to GMOs;

- increased aging (especially in the liver);

- dysregulation of genes associated with cholesterol synthesis, insulin regulation, cell signaling, and protein formation;

- and dangerous changes to the liver, kidney, spleen, and gastrointestinal system.[170]

Meanwhile, Roundup Ready crops were also creating "resistant" super-weeds, something that was harder to deny, so 2,4-D Ready crops were engineered to replace them. These crops would survive one of the most powerful herbicides ever made, so powerful that it even contains (as one of two principal ingredients) the infamous "Agent Orange" defoliant used in the Vietnam War, which has been associated with many negative human health effects. Even if human beings are able to survive the effects of exposure to 2,4-D, it is doubtful whether soil will. Soil treated with this poison repeatedly is dead, exactly the opposite of what soil should be to produce wholesome and nourishing crops. Crops need the bacteria in soil to convert minerals to a form usable by the plant. Dead soil cannot do this.

At the same time that the FDA tries to remain as silent as possible about GMOs, the US Department of Agriculture and other parts of the US government are doing everything they can to promote them. The USDA under both George W. Bush and Obama has sought to accelerate what is already an automatic rubberstamp for new GMO products, to "deregulate" them (including grasses such as alfalfa that cannot be restricted to the planted area), and to provide immunity from lawsuits over the spread of GMO crops to adjoining organic farms. Immunity from lawsuit was especially ironic. For years, GMO producers had threatened, intimidated, sued, and in every imaginable way attempted to bully adjoining farmers. If any of the patented seeds drifted and were found on the neighboring farm, that farmer would be charged with "theft." The clear message: buy the patented seeds or face destruction through legal costs. Remarkably, courts were buying this specious argument. But finally the persecuted began to counter-sue successfully, and the USDA immediately rushed to provide legal immunity to the GMO producers in the form of an insurance policy that organic farmers would have to buy and that would be their only available form of compensation.[171]

Other arms of the US government work just as hard for GMO companies. The patent office supplies the all-important legal protections for new GMO products, in effect creating enforceable monopolies. Even the State Department pitches in. Wikileaks documents revealed the US Ambassador to France, Craig Stapleton, appointed by George W. Bush, sent the following message back to the State Department:

> Europe is moving backward not forwards on this [GMO] issue with France playing a leading role, along with Austria, Italy, and even the [European] Commission.... Moving to retaliation will make clear that the current path has real costs to EU interests and could help strengthen European pro-biotech voice.

> Country team Paris recommends that we calibrate a target retaliation list that causes

some pain across the EU since this is a collective responsibility, but that also focuses in part on the worst culprits. The list should be measured rather than vicious and must be sustainable over the long term, since we should not expect an early victory. . . .

What did Europe do to deserve this? In short, it had the effrontery to ban GMO products because of safety concerns. This precaution on Europe's part meant that the vast uncontrolled GMO experiment on human beings would be concentrated in the US and some other countries. As Stapleton's message revealed, US embassies were instructed to counter this by a wide variety of means, including the circulation of claims that GMO crops produced higher yields or were otherwise helping to feed the world, claims that were demonstrably false.[172]

In 2012, GMO companies responded to the inconvenience of court hearings by quietly inserting a rider (amendment) into the fiscal year 2013 House Agriculture Appropriations bill stripping federal courts of the authority to halt the sale or sowing of GMO crops while USDA undertakes an environmental assessment, and further authorizing the Secretary of USDA to allow sale and sowing even if the crop is found to pose environmental risks. This rider was discovered and provoked wide protests, but was eventually passed as a completely unrelated item in the March 2013

Continuing Resolution funding the government for six months. Note that all of this is concerned with environmental risks only, because the USDA has no further jurisdiction. Only the FDA has the power to address health risks—but does not choose to do so.

Although we have chosen to focus on the remarkable revolving door career of Michael Taylor at the FDA and Monsanto, because it has potentially affected the future health of hundreds of millions of people, stories like his are not uncommon. A *Chicago Tribune* article from 2012 is headlined: Chemical Firms Champion New EPA (Environmental Protection Agency) Expert. It describes how Todd Stedeford worked at the EPA from 2004–2007 under the George W. Bush Administration, then joined chemical firm Albemarle Corp. While at Albemarle, which makes flame retardants, he defended chemicals used in many products and even suggested that the standard set by the EPA for flame retardants was 500x too high. Having returned to the EPA in 2011, under President Obama, he is now "in charge of a . . . program studying whether dozens of industrial chemicals, including flame retardants, are too dangerous."[173] One must ask: what was the EPA thinking when it made this appointment?

Bill Ruckelshaus, twice EPA head, once said that "at EPA you work for a cause that is beyond self-interest. . . . You're not there for the money, you are there for something beyond yourself."[174] But on leaving the EPA, he himself became a Monsanto director. Meanwhile the Geneva-based Covalence group placed Monsanto dead last on a list of 581 global companies ranked by their reputation for ethics.[175]

12

Washington's Plantation System

BEFORE DISCUSSING HOW Big Food operates today, let's take a moment to look back at how agriculture operated in the US South in the late 19th and early 20th centuries. Viola Goode Liddell, daughter of a cotton salesman, described the system:

> When an [Alabama] Black Belt farmer sent his cotton down river to Mobile, he . . . had to take what he was given and be satisfied. . . . The big cotton dealers [had financed him and] the weighing . . . and grading of the cotton was . . . at their discretion. . . . Furthermore, these cotton kings either bought

outright or went into partnership with fer-
tilizer houses, feed and implement stores,
and wholesale groceries, so that [the grow-
ers] ... had to buy everything they needed
for running their farms and for advancing
their tenants from specified concerns. ...
The tenant farmer and sharecropper [were
at the bottom of the chain] ... but ... the
landlord ... had the same kind of rope
around his neck that was about the tenant's, except it was bigger and stronger and
more likely to choke him to death. ...[176]

As this passage attests, agriculture was a controlled
market in the late 19th and early 20th century South,
and it remains controlled today, although the system
is not the same. Control now lies in the hands of the
government and its private, industrial farming and
food processing cronies, today's equivalent of yester-
day's "big dealers."

These cronies, including Monsanto and other giant
food concerns, dominate food and farm policy at the
White House, USDA, FDA, and EPA. The regulators seem to prefer big firms because they are easier
to manage than thousands of little family farms and
businesses. Besides, they provide lucrative jobs, other
emoluments, and campaign contributions. The giant
food firms in turn like the system because new and
small competitors are ill-equipped to handle legal

and lobbying expenses and uncertainties, not to mention often hostile regulators intent on preserving monopolies and quasi-monopolies for their friends.

More than in other industries, prices are government controlled, even though economists on both right and left sides of the political spectrum agree that direct price controls are counter-productive. For a quarter century beginning in 1958, the government did not allow Safeway to reduce food prices.[177] That eventually changed, but some retail food prices are still directly controlled, notably milk.

Have dairy farmers benefited from this? It would seem not. Most dairy farmers over the years have been driven out of business, and the pace of dairy farm failure accelerated after 2008. USDA rules and regulations, especially the Pasteurized Milk Ordinance (PMO), have both stifled innovation and concentrated production into huge factory farm dairies, many located in California, whose arid climate makes it easier to pack thousands of animals into a small space. As a direct result, milk is less and less available locally and must be shipped across the country. This is not only costly and wasteful of energy; it also means the milk must be ultra-pasteurized for long shelf life, which makes it less nutritious. It is also illogical to concentrate dairy, which requires prodigious amounts of water, in the water-scarce West.

Over the years, tightening government regulations have shut down most local, small slaughter houses. It is more convenient for USDA inspectors to visit a few giant operations. This and other policies have also encouraged the growth of huge factory farms for chickens, eggs, hogs, and other animal products. These operations, usually called Confined Animal Feeding Operations (CAFOs), squeeze animals into smaller and smaller spaces, creating pitiful conditions, mountains of excrement, and uncontrollable sanitation problems. Contamination and outbreaks of food-borne illnesses are invariably traced to these CAFOs, but when the government responds, it does so by creating new regulations and expenses for small, local operations, which are not the source of the problem, so that even more of them are driven out of business.

The latest government spasm along these lines was the Food Safety Act of 2011, a bill that was passed by legislative legerdemain. A bill passed by the House was taken up by the Senate, the old language excised, the new Senate food safety legislation dropped in, in order that the Senate could pretend to be acting on a House bill, as required by procedure. Both chambers ultimately approved the new language.[178] The Act as initially written called for sizable fees payable to government by even tiny food operations. This did not survive, but for the first time the FDA got direct legal authority over individual family farms. Prior to this legislation, farmers of all sizes had to answer (only!) to the USDA, Defense Department Corps of Engineers, EPA, and state regulators.

The FDA knows little or nothing about farming. But this new authority may eventually put FDA inspectors on the farm, and if so the agency will want farms to be large scale and limited in number. This is the FDA's pattern. For a time, the Agency banned the import of French cheeses that were not heavily pasteurized, a step inconsistent with making the finest cheese. Then a few very large French cheese makers were allowed to export to the US. Smaller, family, and artisanal cheesemakers were not.

Among the regulations that small farmers already face are Clean Water Act requirements governing waterways and wetlands. The Act exempts agriculture. That sounds simple, but it is not. If a farmer wants to build a pond, he had better get the Corps of Engineer's permission. This can be enormously costly and time consuming.

There is not even a settled, legal definition of a wetland. One Corps office may advise to file form X; another may say, no, file form Y. What if the farmer later wants to sell fishing rights to the pond? No, that is not farming. The Corps can hit you with massive fines and require both the removal of the pond and restoration of the landscape just as it was. Almost any step a small farmer or rancher takes may be creating serious legal liabilities. Who has the money or legal assistance to sort it all out or the paperwork to prove compliance? Once you have made a mistake, the government can threaten jail.

The US Department of Labor in 2011 decided to ban children working on family farms. Faced with criticism, they said they would exempt "family" farms. But what exactly did they mean by that? They meant, it turned out, farms directly owned by the child's parents in their own name. Farms held in a family partnership or LLC were not deemed "family" farms. Finally in 2012, USDL backed off, but the secretary said she was disappointed at this outcome and the Agency might return to the issue in the future.[179]

If the US government really wants to protect children, why did it approve pizza as a vegetable under the School Lunch Program?[180] Why does it also dump into school lunches poor quality meat that has been irradiated (nuked) to eliminate bacterial contamination? Why did Congress specifically override efforts to restrict greasy french fries in school lunches? In each case, the reason was that powerful food companies wanted to sell pizza or potatoes, and the government wanted to dump its own surplus meat, and school children were an easy target. Producers of sugar-laden food even pay "rebates" (subsidies) to food service companies supplying school lunches in order to encourage processed over fresh food.

For years the federal government advised people to stop smoking, but subsidized the growers of tobacco. That only ended by paying tobacco allotment holders lump sums to buy them out. Now the government warns people to cut back on sugar consumption, but supports sugar growers with price supports and tariffs against foreign sugar. The Fanjul family of Florida owns much of the domestic sugar production; members of the family are well known political donors who have contributed more than $1.8 million to politicians over the years.[181] The Fanjuls' sugar, sucrose, which appears on kitchen shelves, is actually far less ubiquitous than the high fructose syrup derived from corn which the government also heavily subsidizes. This is an important product of Archer Daniels Midland (ADM), another large-scale source of federal of political campaign funds ($495,000 2011–August 20, 2012).

Government farm subsidies are notoriously skewed toward larger farm operators: $1 dollar of every $2 dollars goes to the top 4%; $ 8 dollars of every $10 to the top 15%.[182] Some of these subsidies even go abroad. In order to avoid trade sanctions under World Trading Organization (WTO) rules, the US government pays $147 million a year to Brazilian cotton producers, so that it can continue to subsidize US cotton producers.[183] There is also the usual toll from fraud or inattention. Over the first ten years of the 2000s, more than $1 billion was paid to deceased farmers, a fifth of them dead for at least seven years.[184]

Payments are not only highly concentrated in terms of recipients. They are also highly concentrated by crop: 90% went to support just five crops: corn, wheat, soybeans, cotton, and rice; 30% to corn alone. US PIRG, a consumer organization, noted about this:

> We're handing out taxpayer subsidies to big agribusinesses to help subsidize junk food. Huge, profitable corporations like Cargill and Monsanto are pocketing tens of billions in taxpayer dollars, and turning subsidized crops into junk food ingredients including high fructose corn syrup . . . at a time when one in three kids is overweight or obese, and obesity-related diseases like diabetes are turning into an epidemic. . . .[185]

> If [federal] agricultural subsidies went directly to [taxpayers] to allow them to purchase food, each of America's 144 million taxpayers would be given $7.36 to spend on junk food and 11 cents with which to buy apples each year—enough to buy 19 Twinkies but less than a quarter of one Red Delicious apple apiece.[186]

US PIRG's chose this example because most of the subsidized crops are found in Twinkies, but among fresh produce, the only significant subsidy goes to apples.

In the summer of 2012, severe drought in the US Midwest drove up the cost of corn, and even threatened to create animal feed shortages. But there was no real shortage of feed corn. Because of the government's ethanol mandate, over 40% of annual corn production is diverted into car fuel. In a normal year, only 36% goes for animal feed, and even less, 24%, for human consumption. Moreover, no one—other than corn producers—likes the ethanol mandate. Environmentalists have long documented that ethanol fuel produces more carbon and smog, not less.

2012 corn animal feed shortages provided the perfect opportunity for the Obama administration to pull the ethanol mandate and subsidy. At the time, this mandate was driving up the cost of corn, the cost of fuel, the cost of animal feed, and would shortly drive up the cost of meat. What did the president actually do? He traveled to Iowa in August of the election year to announce that the federal government would buy up $100 million worth of pork, $50 million of chicken, and $20 million of lamb and catfish.[187] So, an additional federal subsidy was piled on top of all the existing ones, with very little likelihood that it would actually help the meat producers.

Does the government really think it should be interfering with meat prices in order to correct the mess it has made in corn prices? If so, perhaps the old Soviet central planners should be brought in to give us some advice about how to go about it?

Part Five

Crony Medicine

13

Soviet-Style Healthcare Pricing

JOHN GOODMAN OF Southern Methodist University is the leading US analyst of what is commonly called healthcare, which employs one in ten American workers.[188] He asks us to imagine for a moment a grocery store run along healthcare industry lines.[189] In this case, he notes:

- Product prices will not be posted.

- The price will vary even within the same store, depending on who is buying and paying.

- You won't be able to shop evenings or weekends.

- If you need something, it probably won't be there in the store. You may be told to come back days or weeks later.

- Even if you find the item, you may have a long wait to be able to buy it.

- If you want to charge your purchase, it won't be at an automated machine; the transaction may be rejected; the necessary records may be missing; someone from outside the store will have to approve the amount of the purchase. Since this all takes time, you may not be able to charge at all.

- You won't have the right to return anything. Even defective merchandise will not be reimbursed. As a result there will be no incentive to maintain product quality.

- Your degree of satisfaction will not matter much to the store. What will count is the satisfaction of third party payers, and the store will focus on how to get the most from their formula. If the third party payer formula says you may not buy cherry pie and ice cream on the same day, you may grumble, but most likely you will have to return to get what you want.

- There will be very few brands to guide you in your selection. Labels and quantities will be all over the map, so direct comparison shopping will be impossible.

- Your chief protection against injury or death from what you buy will be hiring a lawyer to sue. These suits will in turn greatly increase the cost of the food you buy.

- The purchase of many food items will require permission from a licensed professional. The professional, fearing a suit, will require you to buy items you do not need or want.

We could go on and on in this vein, but the point is clear. The grocery industry somehow manages to organize thousands of products, many coming from thousands of miles away, and have them on the shelves whenever you want them, at prices that in total represent a small proportion of national income. There is also tremendous consumer choice. Yes, many grocery and drug stores seem to be primarily junk food stores, but this is the consumer's choice, and there are health food stores as well.

By contrast, the healthcare industry is a mess. Costs keep rising, consuming more and more of national income; quality of service keeps declining; and outcomes are surprisingly poor. It is not widely known, but research in respected medical journals suggests that healthcare mistakes are the leading cause of death in the US, ahead even of cancer and heart disease.[190] John Goodman points out that the free price system (he calls it the market system) delivers efficiency, the elimination of waste and unnecessary work, falling prices, and increasing quality. So why have we taken prices, much less free prices, out of healthcare? Why has "every developed nation . . . so completely suppressed normal market forces in healthcare that no one ever sees a real price for anything?"[191] And why is this happening at the very same time that 30 countries have partly or fully privatized their retirement pension systems, having concluded that government control is a bad idea, that it has just led to unsustainable Ponzi schemes like the US Social Security system.[192]

Of course, many people believe that healthcare prices are inappropriate because service of this kind should be free. The word free in this context is misleading, since taxes (or government borrowing) would pay for it, but free at least in the sense that government provides it to the consumer at no incremental cost. Even this formulation turns out to be wrong. There would be many costs to the consumer, costs that go far beyond taxes.

As is often pointed out, if healthcare is free, demand will surely rise. And if supply (doctors, hospitals, etc.) does not rise too, costs will soar. This is one of the reasons that government, once it starts subsidizing, usually subsidizes more and more. As demand steadily rises without a commensurate rise in supply, government responds with further subsidies, with the same result again, in a vicious circle.

The only reliable way to bring costs down in any sector of the economy is to increase supply. And it must be the right kind of supply. There is no way that government can discover what supply is needed, or even define supply. Only free prices can be expected to solve the problem of what is needed where in order to meet consumer demand in a rational way.

John Goodman notes:

> The problem of the Soviet economy writ large is exactly the same problem we have in our healthcare system. Should we train one more doctor? Or would our money be better spent training a nurse or two? If we choose the doctor, should she be a primary care physician? Or an internist? Or some other specialist? How on earth would anybody ever know? No one in healthcare ever sees a real price. No patient. No doctor. No employee. No employer. In the absence of real prices, we have no way of knowing the marginal value of one more doctor, one more nurse, one more technician, or one more anything.[193]

Not only are free prices needed to sort out the number of doctors and nurses. We also need a free price system to sort out their respective roles. At present, the American Medical Association, a physician's group, leans on government to restrict severely the things that nurses are allowed to do, and thus creates an artificial, government-enforced monopoly for its member physicians. This is only one example of how government controls thwart efficiency. To experience the full Alice-in-Wonderland quality of government-controlled medicine, one need only take a look at the bizarre Medicare payment system:

- Medicare sets a payment schedule for 7,500 separate tasks, varied by location and other factors. As John Goodman points out, this translates into the government controlling about 6 billion medical price transactions at any one time, none of which make any economic sense.[194]

- Hospitals are paid as much as three times more for many procedures than private physicians. For example, Dr. Thomas Lewandowski, a Wisconsin cardiologist, found that he received $150 for an echocardiogram versus $400 if done by a hospital employee; $60 for a stress test versus $180; and $10 for an electrocardiogram versus more than $25. Eventually, he, like many other physicians, gave up and sold his practice to a hospital. When he did, he also agreed to follow hospital guidelines for treatment that limited his independence and also agreed to see more patients per day.[195]

- The Medicare coverage and price schedule is so complex that if you call Medicare for instruction, and ask different personnel, you will get widely varying answers, as documented by a number of studies. But if a physician makes a mistake and bills for something not covered, he or she has committed fraud, punishable by jail. Moreover, one cannot rely on advice from Medicare personnel as a legal defense. It is not surprising that a significant number of doctors, estimated at 15%[196] but much higher in some areas, refuse to treat Medicare patients, and the number is likely to grow rapidly.

■ Medicare does not pay for phone calls, email, or showing patients how to do things for themselves. So these tools, which have revolutionized other service professions, are rarely used.

■ Medicare also refuses to pay for blood tests not connected to a specific illness. The use of blood tests to identify health problems before they emerge has the potential to revolutionize medicine, but Medicare says no.

■ Doctors and patients can also benefit from computer and cell phone applications or "apps" such as those which monitor blood pressure and send the information to the doctor. Will Medicare pay for them? No, unless the "app" has been taken through the FDA approval process at vast cost. Meanwhile the FDA says it is concerned about the proliferation of medical software for cell phones, and may crack down on anyone selling it without approval. The same applies to electronic sensors. And what about genetic testing? With a few exceptions, Medicare will not pay for that either, even if it has been taken through the FDA. In this way, American healthcare is essentially frozen in time, unable to take advantage of any new technology whose owner has not paid millions, or hundreds of millions, to get government approval, or in some cases, even after such approval.

- If an elderly patient comes to a doctor with more than one problem, Medicare will not pay the doctor for treating more than one problem at a time. So if the patient has high blood pressure and also diabetes, there must be two appointments. Of course it is not quite that simple. A specialist may be given half pay for treating a second problem at the same time, unlike a family doctor who gets nothing. Who makes up these strange rules? Do the specialists have more lobbyists in Washington?

- During the campaign to pass the Affordable Care Act (ACA), the Obama administration ran ads trumpeting the right of seniors under Medicare to a "free medical checkup" and encouraging them to make an appointment. In actuality, this "checkup" is a "wellness exam" in which the doctor's office measures the patient's height, weight, body mass, and blood pressure. The doctor may also listen to the heart with a stethoscope through clothing. That's it. What a wonderful use of patients' and medical office time![197]

Those arguing for government run healthcare, despite its inability to control costs or improve quality, or even to tell that truth, often insist that healthcare is a unique case, unlike other industries. If you cannot afford a fancy house, they say, then you can live more modestly. But if you cannot afford an operation, you may die, and no just society will allow people to die for lack of money.

This argument does not hold up to close inspection. Food, clothing, shelter, even transportation are all more, not less, essential than healthcare. We recognize this: the government gives out free food stamps in an effort to ensure that no one starves. The food stamp program is far from perfect. There appears to be a good deal of fraud. The government subsidy may be used to buy junk food or even cigarettes or liquor. But at least recipients of food stamps are not herded into special food-aid or food-care programs run like Medicaid or Medicare. They are instead given cards which function as cash in regular stores, and there is no legal prohibition against the customer adding his or her cash to complete the transaction, as there is in Medicaid and Medicare.

Here's another, related question: given that we generally need food more urgently than healthcare, why does the government encourage employers, through tax deductions, to pay for healthcare but not food? Why is it that businesses failing to offer free food are not accused of "starving" their workers? The answer is part of American history. During World War II, wage and price controls prevented employers from raising worker's wages. Workers being scarce, big employers persuaded government to give them an advantage over small businesses by allowing them to offer tax deductible health coverage as a recruitment tool. Small businesses and sole proprietors, which could not usually afford to offer this benefit, thus had to compete on a less than level playing field. And unemployed or retired people lost the health deduction for healthcare completely. Does any of this make sense?

Peter Orszag, President Obama's first Budget Director, offers another reason why, in his opinion, healthcare is a unique industry, not actually comparable to food, shelter, clothing, transportation, and other necessities. Although some people eat more food than others, the difference is not great, and free market prices can effectively discipline our choices. But in healthcare, only 5% of customers take half of all the services. Half the customers use only 3% of the services.[198] This being so, how can giving consumers choices among free prices both improve quality and bring down prices?

This argument may sound convincing. Perhaps healthcare really is unique and not subject to market solutions? But let's inquire a little further. The 5% of customers who use 50% of medical services are not the same people every year. They are, by and large, different people. And since these costs could hit almost anyone, there is no real argument for a government take-over of healthcare, just an argument for a sensible private insurance program which will cover only unexpected and unpredictable catastrophic events, not unlike the fire insurance that most people take out on homes, without covering the more predictable features of home ownership such as routine heating/cooling maintenance or periodic repainting.

There is another, even more fundamental reason to reject any argument that healthcare is too unique to be provided, like other goods and services, by a free price system. The reason is that, at any given time, nobody really knows what healthcare is or should be. Markets do not just provide goods or services. Before they do that, they first define what these goods and services will be. Then, having arrived at some definition of them, they must keep changing the definition in response to consumer preferences and signals. In a market system, consumers over time have the final say about how to define and continually redefine the product through their purchase decisions.

Alex Marshall has written a *Bloomberg View* editorial entitled "Healthcare Will Become a Right Just Like Water?" He notes that government provides free water, at least in cities. Why should healthcare be any different? We have already noted that water (or anything else from the government) is not really free. But let's not worry about that. The real problem with Marshall's idea is that water is water (most of the time) while healthcare has to be defined by someone.

Healthcare isn't brought up from a well. It is an idea that has to be fleshed out to become an actual service. Then someone needs to deliver that service.

Automobiles do not come out of the ground either. Consumers decide what they will look like and how they will operate by buying or refusing to buy specific models. The same is true about computers. If the government-provided automobiles or computers for free, this would all change. Then the government would decide what an automobile or computer is.

If government decided what an automobile or computer is, you can be sure that big companies making these products would lobby government very actively to get the answer they want. These companies would command a lot of money to put into the political process. In the case of automobiles, the labor unions would also have a considerable say.

How much influence would the consumer have? Not much. And how much influence would new or small companies with innovative new ideas have? Most likely zero. In any case, a product provided free by government would be heavily regulated, and regulators don't much like change, so there would not be any point to further innovation.

What if government provides health insurance? It is the same. Government-provided health insurance means government defined health insurance which means government defined healthcare. And government defined healthcare becomes politicized, stagnant, with even major errors hard to change. Above all, it becomes subject to importuning by special interests whose main concern is profit, not health.

So, when Marshall concludes by saying "The arc of history suggests that eventually Americans will accept the right to healthcare," we can only respond by asking: What healthcare? Whose idea of healthcare? Influenced by whom?—because healthcare is not at all like water.*

We see more or less the same flaw in another Peter Orszag proposal: that doctors should be exempted from the crushing cost of liability insurance so long as they follow "evidence-based medicine."[199] Is Orszag even familiar with the technical definition of "evidence-based medicine?" It means treatments that are supported by numerous double blind placebo controlled human trials. By that definition, as little as 5% of medicine is "evidence-based."

Moreover, even human trials, when they can be used at all, often prove to be wrong. Or, more subtly, they turn out to be right for some people with a certain genetic makeup and wrong for others with a different genetic makeup, or right for one age or gender and wrong for another. People differ, and one-size-fits-all is not good medicine.

---

* Even water of course is not necessarily just water. If it were a completely undifferentiated commodity, people would not be choosing bottled water from the Fiji islands over other bottled water.

"Evidence-based medicine" sounds like something everyone would want. But in practice, it would all be defined by the government. This is the same government that is so easily influenced by wealthy special interests, the same government that, being a bureaucracy, is notoriously averse to change, the same government that, being free of the carrot and stick of profit and loss, has little reason to change or accept change, or to listen to consumer preferences.

Democratic elections are fine things, but they usually turn on a handful of issues, or on judgments of personality or character. They are not fit instruments for disciplining government in its choice of what is medically "evidence-based" and what is not. It is much better to let ideas of what is "evidence-based" and what is not compete in a marketplace of opinions and services, not to centralize and thus freeze them.

Here is a simple example. Mammograms are supposed to catch breast cancer while it is still treatable. Several politicians, most notably Hillary Clinton, have campaigned in favor of mammography as a fundamental female right. But mammograms involve radiation, and the extra radiation may eventually cause breast cancer. In addition, there are many false positive readings, which even if not false may lead to surgery or radiation of small tumors that would have disappeared on their own. The radiation may also damage the heart, which cannot be shielded when radiating the breast.

Given all these factors, should mammography be a political decision, much less a political campaign issue or political right? And what about the manufacturers of the equipment, which is very expensive, or the doctors making large incomes from the procedure? Will they not influence what has become a political process? If mammography proves to be more harmful than helpful, how will we ever replace it with thermography or other techniques, so long as vested interests stand in the way and the consumer has little voice?

14

Doubling Down on Crony Medicine

THE MOST CENTRAL objections to the Affordable Care Act (Obamacare), are that it:

- Was born behind closed doors in meetings with special interests;

- Takes a medical system in which consumers only control 12 cents of every dollar spent[200] and further diminishes consumer control;

- Puts government even more in charge of defining what health, health insurance, and medicine are;

- And thereby increases the influence of special interests and corporate lobbyists on medicine.

There are other, more specific, objections as well:

- Depending on specific regulations, ACA may eventually abolish high deductible health insurance policies, which give consumers the most choice and control.

- ACA requirements will cost employers of 50 or more employees a minimum of $2.28 per hour per employee (and $5.89 an hour per employee if a family is included). By 2014, the year the Act takes effect, this means that a minimum wage of $7.25 per hour will be increased to $9.53–$13.14 an hour or as much as $27,331 a year. This is a huge disincentive for small businesses to add a 50th employee, and would be further exacerbated if the minimum wage is raised to $9, as President Obama has proposed. Similar rules in France have led to a proliferation of 49-employee businesses. The same is already starting to happen in the US.

- The definition of a 50-employee firm includes part-time employees counted on a full-time employee basis. But just to make it more complex, the employer penalty is based on full-time employees only. This has created incentives for firms to stop hiring full-time employees and reduce full-time employees to part time. It has also led to "work sharing." One Burger King franchise will employ a former full-time employee part time and send him or her to another franchise for more part-time hours.

- Among employers of 50 or more, the rule has also led to the elimination of minimum wage jobs, for example in drugstores where self-checkout machines are rapidly replacing counter clerks, a trend that picked up sharply after passage of the legislation. In the end, the combination of employer-mandated healthcare with other ACA requirements will prove to be a massive job disrupter and killer.[201]

- Twenty new or higher taxes, fees, and fines, in addition to the increase in direct employee costs, will drain money that might otherwise have gone into hiring a new employee. In this environment, employers will ask existing employees to work longer hours. They will try to avoid committing to a new full-time employee.

- One of the biggest of the new taxes, an increase of the Medicare payroll tax from 2.9% to 3.8%, which applies to all taxable income, will not even be used to fund Medicare. Although called a Medicare tax, it will be used to fund other provisions of the ACA, even though Medicare is understood to be facing eventual bankruptcy as more and more retirees are supported by fewer and fewer younger workers.

- A majority of the newly insured under the ACA will be brought into the Medicaid program. This makes little sense when existing Medicaid participants are often unable to find a doctor who will accept Medicaid payments, and when many states are ruthlessly cutting back on what Medicaid covers. The Act also states that if you are eligible for Medicaid, you cannot buy any other insurance or supplementary insurance on the new official exchanges, and it is not expected that any insurance will be available off the exchanges. Medicaid in effect becomes a government-mandated ghetto.

- There is also a nonsensical anomaly about the Medicaid provisions of ACA. If your state agrees to expand Medicaid as envisioned by the Act, everyone up to 138% of the poverty line is forced into Medicaid. If your state opts out, as the Supreme Court has made possible, and your income is from 100%-138% of the poverty line, you luck out, because you get private insurance at a highly subsidized rate, and only have to spend 2% of your income. If you are below the poverty line, only your children will definitely qualify for Medicaid, so you may continue to have no insurance.[202]

- Another anomaly is that if you are not employed by someone else, and fall into the 100–138% of poverty income zone, you get the rich government subsidy, worth as much as $20,000. But if you are covered through an employer, your employer does not get this subsidy.[203] That being the case, your employer will logically drop your insurance and pay a penalty.

- ACA will spell out exactly what each health insurer will offer in coverage. So how can an insurer try to tip the scales to ensure profitability? The answer is to attract patients who are in better health and avoid patients in chronically poor health. The system is essentially set up so that your insurer will want to get rid of you if you need a lot of services—not exactly a consumer friendly approach. Would you want to go to a grocery store or restaurant that you knew in advance did not want your business? Will this approach actually help those who need help the most? Of course not.[204]

- The Act also requires that 80% of insurance fees go to patient care. But it doesn't prevent some of this money going for services that will attract customers in better, rather than worse health, for example services that will appeal to upscale customers, who tend to be in better health, compared to downscale customers. So long as the 80% expenditure threshold is met, the insurance company is under no compunction to provide an excellent level of service for the sickest and neediest patients.

- The 80% of expenditure threshold does not include any money spent on preventing fraud. So government, which is notoriously unable to detect or prevent fraud, will now discourage private companies from doing anything about it either.

- The ACA requires insurers to offer a long list of so-called preventive medicine measures with no copayment or deductible, so that they are "free" for the patient. In many cases, the preventive measures are of dubious value. We have already mentioned some of the problems associated with mammograms. Another example is cholesterol screening for children and adolescents, a group who especially need cholesterol, because it is the basic building block of hormones. Putting teenagers, whose diet may be poor, on statins, prescription drugs that may damage muscles and that deplete CoQ10, essential for your body and heart, is only good for the drug companies, not the teenagers. But this is what teenager cholesterol screening typically produces.

- Another problem with the "free" preventive measures required under the ACA is that if everyone "took advantage" of them, it has been estimated that the average primary care physician would have to spend full time delivering these services alone, with zero time left over for people who are actually sick.[205]

- The ACA proposes to control the growth of medical expenses by promoting demonstration projects or lessons from alleged exemplary practices such as the Cleveland Clinic or Mayo Clinic. But there are already no lack of demonstration projects, and none of them, nor the alleged exemplary practices, have demonstrated a replicable way to reduce the cost of medical services.

- The Act also reduces fees paid to doctors under Medicare and mandates that future Medicare expenses grow no faster than overall GDP (US Gross Domestic Product). These fee caps are price controls, and price controls do not work outside of a wartime environment. Controlling prices from on high just leads to a reduction in supply, so that prices rise rather than fall, or goods become unavailable at any price.

This is what happened when the government of the doomed monarch Louis XVI in 18th century France tried to control the price of grain to help the poor. Its decrees backfired and led to mass starvation. Prices controls leading to price increases are already quite evident in the US healthcare sector, and price increases will only get worse as the government sets more and more prices in an effort to drive them down. The only effective way to get prices down is to increase supply, and this requires free prices. John Goodman explains this further:

> Doctors are the only professionals in our society who are not free to repackage and re-price their services. If demand changes, if technology changes, if new information becomes available, every other professional

is free to offer a different bundle of services to the market and charge a different price. It is precisely this freedom that leads accountants, lawyers, engineers, architects—and, yes, even economists—to compete for customers based on price and quality (and in the process increase the availability of services).[206]

- The philosophy behind the ACA not only rejects free prices; it also rejects their corollary, profits. In his October 3, 2012 televised debate against GOP presidential candidate Mitt Romney, President Obama said that government-provided medical insurance services, notably Medicare, are cheaper than private insurance. This is inaccurate.[207] Even more importantly, the president said that government-provided medical insurance should be cheaper than private medical insurance, because it does not have the added expense of a profit margin. This shows a complete ignorance of economics. Even Karl Marx, the father of Communism, acknowledged (in the 1848 *Communist Manifesto* of all places) that profits do not increase costs. Instead they provide an incentive to drive costs lower and lower.

- In general, the cost reduction ideas imbedded in the ACA are not just ineffective. They also depend on eliminating individual choice from medicine. As Dr. Richard Fogoros has said:

The entire structure of Obamacare is designed specifically to remove important (i.e. costly) medical decisions from the purview of the individual doctor and patient. The role of the doctor is now to relay expert-guided determinations of what is best for the herd down to the level of the individual patient, and to do it in such a way that their patients do not realize that the doctor's recommendations are population-based, and not tailored to their own needs.

John Goodman expands on this:

It's not just the Obama administration, by the way. Underlying an enormous amount of medical research is the idea that we are all alike.

To make up an example, think about a clinical trial in which one group drinks coffee and the other group abstains. Then let's suppose the non-drinkers turn out to have a statistically significantly higher rate of colon cancer. So doctors respond by telling everyone to drink a cup of coffee every morning. This would be called "evidence-based" advice. What's the implicit premise behind all this? That the two groups of people are alike in every important respect

(other than their coffee consumption) and
that the rest of us also are just like the people who've just been tested. I've written before why clinical trials like the one I just
described are absurd. At least the way the
results are used is absurd.[208]

■ One of the principal cost control mechanisms under
the ACA is the establishment of a so-called Independent Payment Advisory Board (IPAB) of 15
appointees. Starting in 2014, recommendations
of the IPAB for controlling Medicare costs must
be enacted into law by Congress by August 15th
of each year. If Congress fails to do this, and fails
to pass other cost saving approaches expected to
yield an equivalent saving, the IPAB recommendations automatically become law.

Provisions governing IPAB get even more interesting. Congress can repeal the IPAB provision only
during a seven-month period in 2017 and only by a
three-fifths vote. After that, it cannot be repealed,
nor IPAB rulings altered. This in effect gives IPAB
law-making authority equal to Congress, which
violates the Constitution, in addition to trying to
control future Congresses, which would also seem
to be illegal.[209]

We have a trial run for the IPAB in the eleven
member commission set up in Massachusetts to
mandate medical price controls. That body not

only has the power to set prices. The law requires that a "medical provider" obtain board commission approval for "any material change to its operations or governance structure."[210] This means, in effect, that the practice of medicine in Massachusetts is frozen without state government approval.

It will be interesting to see how the phrase "material change" will be interpreted. It is a phrase that cannot really be defined for legal purposes. It will be whatever the state government says it is. It could be defined to mean even switching from one drug to another. And if a doctor guesses wrong and fails to get permission, he or she could be in serious legal trouble. Under these circumstances, would you want to practice in Massachusetts? Yet the same could be coming nationally through the federal IPAB.

- ACA also requires that patient records become electronic. This might seem like a good idea until one discovers that up to 800,000 parties may have legal access to your most personal conversations with your doctor. This is mandated under the Federal HIPAA Act of 1996, ostensibly passed to protect patient privacy, but actually removing previous patient privacy protections. It has already been demonstrated how easy it is for hackers to steal electronic records or for "authorized" users to release them inadvertently. Will someone hoping for a public career, or just someone concerned about privacy, ever again confide in the doctor? FBI questionnaires, which must be filled out in order to apply for many federal jobs, already ask if the applicant has seen a psychiatrist in the prior five years. Will the government now verify your answer online?

- Electronic medical records are presented in ACA as a cost-saving device. But it has become increasingly evident that these systems, which include billing as well as patient records, make it easier for doctors and hospitals to increase their billing of Medicare, Medicaid, and the Veteran's Administration. In some instances, as soon as the electronic system has gone in, claims have jumped by as much as 40%. For example, the percentage of the highest-paying claims at Baptist Hospital in Nashville climbed 82 percent in 2010—one year after it began using a software system for its emergency room records. In general, hospitals that received government incentives to adopt EMR showed a 47% rise in Medicare payments from 2006 to 2010, compared with a 32% rise at hospitals that did not receive any government incentives.[211]

- Electronic billing also facilitates fraudulent as well as legitimate billing. An extensive case history of a nonexistent patient can be created in minutes.[212]

- The federal government is mandating and in many cases subsidizing the installation of the new systems, but also making no effort whatever to verify that the systems are working properly, are achieving the desired outcome, and are not being used to defraud the government. A recent Department of Health and Human Services Inspector General report acknowledged as much. Many doctors even report that the new federal requirements are greatly increasing their paperwork, not decreasing it.

- The electronic medical records (EMR) industry pushed for a $25 billion subsidy for their product from the 2009 stimulus bill and got $19 billion. These funds and the subsequent Obamacare EMR mandate particularly benefited three large EMR companies. The annual sales of Allscripts and Epic doubled 2009–2012 while Cerner's increased 60%. The first two companies are close to the Obama administration; the last is not. The then-CEO of Allscripts, Glen E. Tullman, served as the health technology advisor to the Obama campaign in 2008. In 2009, as the stimulus package was being constructed, he visited the president at least seven times, and personally donated over $225,000 to the campaigns of legislators like Sen. Max Baucus (chairman of the Senate Finance Committee) and Jay D. Rockefeller (chairman of the Commerce Committee).[213]

Judith Faulkner, founder and CEO of Epic Systems, a company that stores 40% of the US population's medical data, is described by columnist Michelle Malkin as "[President] Obama's ... billionaire ... medical information czar ... who just happens to be ... a major Democratic contributor."[214] Critics of her firm's platform insist that it represents an outmoded technology and that federal rules are just freezing medical information technology in place, to the advantage of established firms.[215]

- At the present time, it appears that ACA, with its numerous mandates, will increase the cost of private health insurance by thousands of dollars per policy.

- If the Act does cut Medicare reimbursements, as legislated, to levels even lower than Medicaid's, it will drive even more doctors to refuse Medicare patients.

- If the Act does succeed in insuring more people, many of them will be unable to find a doctor, because supply will not have kept pace with demand.[216]

- The Act forces insurers to treat young and old alike. Since young people use relatively few and cheaper medical services, this represents a massive transfer of money from young people, who typically have little money and who must now buy health insurance, to old people, who are on average much better off, and in many cases are actually rich. This is in addition to the diversion of Medicare tax proceeds out of Medicare to fund other provisions of the ACA, which means that young people will face an even bigger shortfall of Medicare funding when they reach retirement age.

15

Big Pharma and FDA: A Marriage Not Made in Heaven*

THE DRUG INDUSTRY at one time was called the patent medicine industry. This is still the more revealing name. Drug companies devote themselves to inventing non-natural molecules for use in medicine. Why non-natural? Because molecules previously occurring in nature cannot, as a rule, be patented. It is essential to develop a patentable medicine; only a medicine protected by a

---

* Parts of this chapter are drawn from Chapter 14 of the author's *Where Keynes Went Wrong: And Why World Governments Keep Creating Inflation, Bubbles, and Busts* (Mt. Jackson, VA: Axios Press, 2011).

government patent can hope to recoup the enormous cost of taking a new drug through the government's approval process.

Getting a new drug through the US Food and Drug Administration (FDA) is not just expensive ($1 billion on average). It also requires having the right people on your side. Drug companies know that they must hire former FDA employees to assist with the process. They also hire leading experts as consultants, some of the same experts who may be called on by the FDA to serve on its screening panels. Direct payments must also be made to support the FDA's budget.

All these financial ties encourage a "wink and a nod" relationship between researchers working for drug companies and regulators, who are often the same people, thanks to the revolving door. As the *Economist* magazine writes:

> Pharmaceutical companies bury clinical trials which show bad results for a drug and publish only those that show a benefit. The trials are often run on small numbers of unrepresentative patients, and the statistical analyses are massaged to give as rosy a picture as possible. Entire clinical trials are run not as trials at all, but as under-the-counter advertising campaigns designed to persuade doctors to prescribe a company's drug.

The bad behavior extends far beyond the industry itself. Drug regulators, who do get access to some of the hidden results, often guard them jealously, even from academic researchers, seeming to serve the interests of the firms whose products they are supposed to police. The French journal *Prescrire* applied to Europe's drug regulator for information on the diet drug rimonabant. The regulator sent back 68 pages in which virtually every sentence was blacked out....

Medical journals frequently fail to perform basic checks on the papers they print, so all sorts of sharp practice goes uncorrected. Many published studies are not written by the academics whose names they bear, but by commercial ghostwriters paid by drug firms. Doctors are bombarded with advertising encouraging them to prescribe certain drugs....[217]

What the *Economist* calls "bad behavior" also spills over from the medical world to the financial world. Just since 2008, 75 people have been charged with trying to profit from inside information about drug approvals or company mergers related to patentable drugs. One of them, an FDA chemist named Cheng Yi Liang with access to the Agency's approval database, pleaded guilty to insider trading on 25 companies for a total gain of $3.78 million over five years. Others with larger resources to invest have made much larger sums. Rod Rothstein, the US Attorney for Maryland who helped prosecute the FDA case, has noted that "healthcare is particularly attractive to criminals because so much turns on government regulatory approval."[218]

Dr. Ben Goldacre, author of *Bad Pharma*, summarizes the entire drug approval process as follows: "[It] is broken. . . . The people you should have been able to trust to fix [the] problems have failed you."[219]

Although the costs of drug approval keep growing, along with the related corruption, the financial payoff for those ultimately winning approval can be astronomical, because approval also brings with it a government-protected monopoly. Only FDA-approved drugs can be prescribed within government programs such as Medicare. Doctors may prescribe unapproved substances outside of Medicare, Medicaid, or the Veteran's Administration, but by doing so risk losing their license to practice. Some approved drugs may be priced as high as $500,000 per year per patient.[220]

The FDA will also discourage, and often ban, substances that might compete with approved drugs. When anti-depression drugs (based on extending the life of a hormone, serotonin, inside the body) were approved, the Agency promptly banned a natural substance, L-Tryptophan, that increased serotonin, even though the natural substance was much cheaper and had long been available. Many years later, after the anti-depression drugs were well established, Tryptophan was finally allowed back, but under restrictions that made it more expensive.

In general, the FDA maintains a resolutely hostile stance toward supplements. It will not allow any treatment claims to be made for them, no matter how much science there is to support it, unless they are brought through the FDA approval process and thus become drugs. The Agency understands that this is a classic "Catch-22." Who can afford to spend up to a billion dollars to win FDA approval of a non-patented substance? The answer is obvious: no one. So the real FDA intent is simply to eliminate any competition for patented drugs, since these drugs pay the Agency's bills.

This FDA policy prevents millions of Americans from hearing about food or supplement remedies that are safer and cheaper than drugs. It hurts the poor and the middle class. But, ironically, it also hurts the rich, even the crony capitalist rich. A national magazine ran a profile of a Wall Street billionaire sitting in his gigantic Connecticut mansion, popping acid blockers for a stomach problem that tormented him. He was totally unaware of research suggesting that most such ailments stemmed from too little acid, not too much, and that a few simple tablets containing hydrochloric acid, one of the cheapest supplements, would probably end his pain.

Why did the billionaire not know this? The answer could not be simpler: crony capitalist drug companies earn huge profits from acid blockers, and along with their friends in government at the FDA, succeed in keeping this information hidden. So there the billionaire sits in his great mansion, unable to enjoy it because of intense stomach pain.

Drug companies and the FDA are not alone in wishing to suppress supplement alternatives to hyper-expensive patented prescription drugs. They have allies among both politicians and doctors. For example, the *Archives of Internal Medicine*, run by the American Medical Association, and supported financially by drug companies, often publishes flimsy studies attacking supplements, and generally ignores the considerable scientific evidence in their favor.

One such study, published October 10, 2011 by University of Michigan researchers, purported to show that taking supplements could shorten your life. It caused a media feeding frenzy, with headlines everywhere. The problem was that this study, like its predecessors, was junk science. The women in the study were asked every six years what they had taken. They were supposed to remember what they had taken for the six-year period. The reports did not have to be specific: the word "multivitamin" could mean anything. Who knows what was taken or even it if was taken? It could also be synthetic or natural.

Those who reported taking "multivitamins" were found over time to be healthier on average than others and to live longer. But the authors of the study, who clearly had an anti-supplement agenda, made numerous "adjustments" attributing the good health to other factors. Once these arbitrary "adjustments" were made, they then concluded that supplements actually made these healthier than average and longer living people unhealthier. Even after the "adjustment," the statistical evidence was weak to nonexistent, but that did not prevent media from all over the world reporting that supplements may hasten your death.

What was behind this? The AMA seems worried about competition for its brand of medicine, which focuses almost exclusively on conventional drugs and surgery. It is especially worried about competition from "integrative" doctors who include advice about food, supplements, and exercise in their practice. The AMA and its affiliates also have a tight relationship with drug companies, and depend on them for financial support in many forms, not just journal advertising. Both the AMA and drug companies thus seem determined to trash supplements and those giving advice on supplements.

How does the media fit into this? Since prescription drug advertising was made legal, the major media have come to depend on it for survival. Without it, most of the companies, already financially hard pressed by internet competition, would face potential bankruptcy. So it was not surprising that the major media would pick up something like the misleading *Archives of Internal Medicine* study and make even more misleading headlines of it.

Are all supplements safe? Of course not. The World Health Organization recently recommended that governments put extra calcium in the public water supply. This is a very bad idea. Genuine medical research suggests that calcium should only be taken with important co-factors such as vitamin D and K2. These help get the calcium into the bones, where it is needed, and keep it out of the heart and circulatory system. As with anything else, good information and common sense are needed to make the best use of supplements. But neither can be expected from the FDA, AMA, or drug company-sponsored media.

The FDA also helps patent drug companies fight off competition from generic (post-patent) drug sellers. Craig R. Smith describes the process:

> Generic drugs are generally much cheaper than patent-protected brand name drugs. But they are still quite expensive, especially given that the active ingredients often cost the manufacturer only a few pennies. And in many cases, there are no generic versions

available even after the patent on the brand name drug has expired.

Here is how the FDA prevents generic drugs from appearing and also keeps the prices of those that do appear high.

Bioequivalence

A major element driving up the cost of generic drugs is bioequivalence testing. If a company wants to manufacture a generic drug, be it a prescription drug like finasteride or an over-the-counter drug like ibuprofen, it must file an Abbreviated New Drug Application (ANDA) with the FDA, even if it is manufactured by others already. The company doesn't have to perform clinical trials for an ANDA, but it does have to show that it's biologically similar, or "bioequivalent," to the original drug. For drugs that are difficult to synthesize, this requirement is important. For most drugs, however, the raw material can be purchased, often from the identical supplier that provides it for the branded drug. To show bioequivalence, the company typically needs to perform human studies that take nearly two years. This can be waived, but it's up to the FDA.

Other Obstacles

Foot dragging: The FDA's Office of Generic Drugs currently has an estimated 1,900 different generic medications awaiting action—and the approval time for generic applications has slowed until it averages more than 26 months.

Name-brand preference: Pharmacy chains get money from drug manufacturers to push their name brands instead of generics. A bill in an earlier Congress (HR 5234) would have made transparent exactly how much money the pharmacies are receiving from pharmaceutical companies to promote drugs still under patent, but it died in committee.

Pay-to-delay: Bayer AG paid rival drug makers nearly $400 million to stay out of the generic Cipro market. By paying competitors to delay their challenges to the patent, they are ensuring an exclusive market for themselves—and the ability to charge whatever they wish.

What We Can Do

We can't really fix this without new legislation, as proposed in 2009 by Bill Faloon of the Life Extension Foundation. Such a bill should allow supplement companies to produce and sell generic drugs. It should also eliminate the red tape (including human trials) that is needlessly preventing generic competition and thus artificially preserving patent drug profits.[221]

Sometimes the FDA or other branches of the federal government deliver opportunities to drug companies, not just protect them from potential competition. For example, federal researchers may develop a chemical which is then licensed to a friendly drug company. Or federal agencies will pay for drug research, or hire drug companies to conduct research. For example, laboratories at the National Cancer Institute are operated by SAIC Inc., a Defense Department contractor which is not a drug producer, but which is a major player in the drug industry, with funding from the US Department of Health and Human Services. The same company operates the government's vaccine production facilities.

Medical marijuana represents another example of how federal agencies assist major drug companies. So long as this was mainly supplied by small time growers and protected by state law, the Drug Enforcement Agency and FDA were unremittingly hostile. But when major drug companies became interested, federal agencies shifted to helping carve out a new monopoly for them.[222]

In effect, then, drug companies are not really private companies competing in an open market. They are government-sponsored enterprises (GSEs) not unlike Fannie Mae or Freddie Mac and the big Wall Street banks and firms. It should not be surprising, therefore, that drug companies spend millions on political lobbying and campaign contributions. Many politicians rely on these campaign contributions and thus have a vested interest in maintaining the drug cartel, even though needlessly high drug costs contribute to soaring medical costs.

Sometimes the relationships are hard to follow. For example, a powerful senator like Majority Leader Harry Reid (D-Nevada) may seem to be at odds with Pharma, but then collect plentiful campaign contributions from drug companies when facing a close race. The drug companies are not only interested in rewarding friends; they also want to keep critics from converting rhetoric into action.

The same principle applies to President Obama. His rhetoric is often populist, as when he condemns those who "gutted regulations and put industry insiders in charge of oversight."[223] But he still expects and accepts drug company and other special interest support.

A more typical case is former Senator Chris Dodd of Connecticut. He sat on the Senate committee overseeing health and for a time was expected to be its next chairman. This enabled him to collect $550,000 from drug companies over the years. In addition, his wife, Jackie Clegg, was paid well, both in cash and stock, to serve on two drug company boards. As noted in an earlier chapter, Dodd and his wife also benefited from a preferential mortgage rate provided by a company, Countrywide Financial, at the heart of the sub-prime home lending scandal that contributed to the Crash of 2008.[224]

The result of all this is that drug companies, ostensibly regulated by the government, have come to rely on the regulators and politicians to feather their mutual nest. Even when today's regulators seem to be cracking down on the drug industry, it is usually not quite what it appears. Merck reached a $650 million settlement with the government to escape charges that it had deliberately overbilled Medicare, Medicaid, and the Veteran's Administration for medicines. This sounded impressive, but it was just a slap on the wrist for the giant drug company. It continued without pause to supply the government with drugs and sold almost a billion dollars' worth in 2010 alone.[225]

The federal government is very careful to avoid charging any leading pharmaceutical company with criminal misconduct, because conviction under current federal law would terminate purchases from that source, and the government is too closely integrated with the drug/vaccine industry to allow that to happen. Thus, when Merck was found to have misled about its painkiller Vioxx, alleged to have caused at least 55,000 deaths (some estimates are much higher), the settlement with plaintiffs reached $4.9 billion. But Merck continued partnering with and selling to government without any interruption or even question.

As government takes over more and more of medicine, through Medicare, Medicaid, Obamacare, and regulatory agencies such as the FDA, it must itself bear more and more monopoly inflated drug costs. Much of this is financed by borrowing from China and other countries, or more recently, by printing money. Not surprisingly, the Chinese have shown themselves to be apt pupils of the crony capitalist US medical system. Among other devices, they have taken to issuing indiscriminate domestic drug patents, so that US firms find it increasingly difficult to enforce their own US patents in China.[226]

Although government now borrows or prints money to pay for healthcare, businesses still pay for a good deal of it, at least for now. Consequently, monopoly-driven high drug prices also reduce business profits, which in turn leads to fewer raises for existing employees, less hiring, and ultimately to higher unemployment. Higher business costs also lead to fewer export sales, which increases the US trade deficit, and so on it goes, with one undesirable and unintended consequence after another.

The bottom line is that the government's semi-socialized drug cartel is wreaking economic havoc. This is an inherently unstable situation. It must eventually give way either to total government price control, which will ultimately fail and be replaced with the rationing of health services themselves, or back to a genuine free price system. In the meantime, investors who continue to regard drug company stocks as high quality "blue chips," safe places to put money for the long term, may have a rude surprise awaiting them.

16

Vaccines: A Crony Capitalist's Dream

JULIE GERBERDING WAS director of the US Center for Disease Control (CDC) from 2002 to 2009. Researchers in this agency patented the technology underlying what became the Gardasil vaccine for genital warts and then licensed it to the drug company Merck on terms that made the two financial partners. This was not in any way unusual.

The US government financially subsidizes and partners with the five leading vaccine makers (GlaxoSmithKline, Merck, Novartis, Sanofi Pasteur, and Wyeth) in numerous ways. Critics find this particularly objectionable because the US government then persuades states to make many of the vaccines a legal requirement for school children. In effect, the developer of the vaccine, not a truly independent third party, decides what works, what is safe, and what will be mandated.

In the testing for Gardasil, it was not compared to an inert placebo (harmless substance) but to an aluminum-based adjuvant that had risk characteristics of its own. Despite this irregularity, approval was "fast tracked" by the CDC.[227] Within months of its launch, Merck was selling over a billion dollars' worth of the vaccine, marketed at that time for teenage girls to prevent cervical cancer, later marketed for teenage boys as well. Three shots were required, the vaccine only worked against some genital warts, not all, and the "adverse events" reported to the CDC began to pile up, including blood clots, neurological disorders, and even deaths, a total of 18,727 reports by the fall of 2011.[228]

By that time, the presidential nominating process was underway, and GOP Congresswoman and candidate Michele Bachmann criticized GOP Texas governor Rick Perry for simultaneously taking campaign money from Merck and issuing an executive order mandating the vaccine in his state. Bachmann was then ridiculed, not only by other politicians, but also by the major media for raising the issue, despite the incontrovertible evidence supporting her position.

A year earlier, Julie Gerberding, who had brought the Gardasil vaccine to market as head of the CDC, left government to become—what else?—president of

Merck Pharmaceutical's vaccine division, maker of the Gardasil vaccine. This new job also put her directly in charge of Merck's Measles, Mumps, Rubella (MMR) vaccine, another controversial shot. One of several concerns with MMR, a possible link to autism in children, has led, not to further scientific research, but rather to media controversy, name-calling, and lawsuits. Dr. Andrew Wakefield, who reported the possible link, found himself charged with unethical behavior, his article was repudiated by the publisher, and the doctor's UK medical license was revoked. Dr. Wakefield subsequently filed suit in the United States, and there is considerable evidence that he is simply a victim of outraged special interests.

Interestingly, Dr. Gerberding was asked on a television show if vaccines in general might cause autism, and did not directly deny it.[229] The Italian Health Ministry also conceded in court that the MMR had caused autism in at least one case.[230] In addition to Dr. Wakefield's lawsuit, another, filed by former vaccine researchers at Merck in 2012, and unrelated to autism, charged that the company fabricated trial results for the MMR, in order to bolster claims of effectiveness.[231] Merck is the sole supplier of this vaccine which had also been approved and promoted by Julie Gerberding's CDC. As of 2012, Merck makes all of the 17 vaccines "recommended" for children by the CDC, and 9 out of 10 "recommended" for adults.

One of the US government's favorite vaccines is supposed to prevent flu. A June 2011 Government Accountability Office report[232] found that the federal departments of Health and Human Services and Defense paid vaccine makers, usually divisions of drug companies, $2.1 billion between August 2004 and March 2011 to subsidize both improved production of the flu vaccine and the development of new versions, including a genetically engineered version utilizing worm viruses and caterpillar ovaries.[233] These funds were part of $7.1 billion authorized by Congress in 2005 to prepare for a dangerous flu pandemic,[234] and additional funding of government-vaccine maker "partnerships" has continued ever since. The "partners" include foreign as well as domestic companies, but building a US plant is a pre-condition for participation.

Does the flu vaccine work? It is hard to be sure because the government refuses to test people who have been vaccinated. There are reasons to think that whatever immunity it confers is very temporary or weak and that it does not actually prevent much flu. In some years, the vaccine is engineered against the wrong strains of the disease.

The US government often mentions "flu deaths" when promoting the vaccine. But, when scrutinized closely, the "flu deaths" appear to be fabricated. Any death associated with respiratory illness is called a "flu death," even when there is no proof of a flu virus and the death has almost certainly been caused by pneumonia, a different illness more commonly associated with bacteria than viruses.

Published research also links the use of stomach acid blockers, a favorite of doctors and a major money maker for Big Pharma, with pneumonia. The problem is that acid in the stomach protects our bodies from pneumonia bugs, and by blocking the acid we put ourselves at risk of many illnesses as well as nutrient deficiencies, especially mineral deficiencies that may lead to weak bones as we age.

Although the US government promotes the idea that its vaccine, and only its vaccine, will protect us from a "flu death," scientific evidence suggests that other preventives may be more powerful by far. A Japanese study found that taking supplemental vitamin D is more effective than the flu shot,[235] and many other studies support this idea as well.[236] Some respected researchers (see www.vitamindcouncil.org) believe that colds and viruses are really symptoms of an underlying lack of vitamin D, caused in part by too much avoidance of sun or living in northern latitudes where the sun's rays are weak in winter, since exposure to sunlight is the main way our bodies make vitamin D. Studies based on blood tests find one third of the US population to be chronically low in D.[237]

Is the US flu shot safe? The answer appears to be no. One independent study found that those inoculated with the seasonal flu vaccine had become more likely to be infected by the more dangerous H1N1 flu virus. An H1N1 vaccine has been associated with several problems, including later narcolepsy. [238] In addition, US flu vaccines usually contain mercury as a preservative. Europe does not allow this, but the US government does. Possibly as a result, one study found a correlation between number of flu shots and incidence of Alzheimer's, a form of elderly dementia. The flu shot also contains "adjuvants," substances intended to make a smaller dose of vaccine more potent, but which are often very dangerous in their own right. Why does the government not only permit, but even encourage, such elements? The stated rationale is that it allows a smaller amount of vaccine per shot, and the government is always worried that enough vaccine will not be available. But is this really a reason to inject children with formaldehyde?

As we have noted, the major media are heavily supported by drug company advertising. For that or other reasons, "adverse events" reported after the flu shot by doctors are almost never mentioned in news reports. The responsible government agencies, primarily the Center for Disease Control, also ignore "adverse events" reported by doctors on the grounds that they are not "peer reviewed research," but also refuse to do the research themselves.

In an effort to shield vaccine makers from legal liability, the US government has set up a "vaccine court," the National Vaccine Injury Compensation Program, funded by a 75-cent-per-shot tax on vaccines. It is by no means easy to get a payment from the program, but there have been payments for serious side effects of the flu shot, including Guillain-Barré Syndrome, acute demyelinating encephalomyelitis, encephalopathy, ventricular fibrillation and cardiac arrest, transverse myelitis, or some combination of these. Even when making these payments, the government routinely adds a disclaimer that "the Respondent (US government) denies injury/death was caused in fact by vaccination." Since claims are only paid with substantial evidence, this disclaimer makes no sense.

In 2011, the US government's Center for Disease Control reported an increase in flu shot "adverse events" taking the form of "febrile seizures," that is, convulsions accompanied by high fever in children,[239] but did not choose to look further or modify its recommendations. Meanwhile the CDC's Government Accountability Office report of the same year (cited earlier) noted the complaint of "stakeholders" (meaning drug companies) that the government was not promoting the shot enough, and that if more people could be talked into getting it, the makers would earn more reliable profits, and thus have more incentive to produce vaccine. Perhaps in response to this, the State of Colorado has ordered all health workers to get the shot or be fired.[240] Other states and hospital systems have followed. Many health workers are very unhappy about this because they are more familiar with mercury-used-as-a-preservative and other issues.

How then can the vaccine industry be described in brief? It is a "partnership" between government and private companies in which government pays for most of the research and may even develop and license the vaccine for its own profit, as it did in the case of Gardasil. The same government then reviews the vaccine for safety and efficacy—and surprise!—approves it.

Private companies produce the vaccine, with heavy government subsidies, and then roll it out to the states, often with a strong federal government recommendation to make it legally mandatory for school children. Once the shot reaches doctor's offices and schools, the manufacturer is shielded from any legal liability for "adverse events." The federal government also generally dismisses any such reports and refuses to investigate them. It also refuses to do follow-up studies to see if the shot is actually conferring much immunity.

All of this is an absolutely shameless example of conflicts of interest, disregard for public safety, and crony medicine at its worst. Yet when challenged by these facts, public health officials in charge of the federal vaccine program may just dismiss critics as "cranks" or "flat-earthers." Bloomberg News in an editorial parrots the line that vaccines are our only hope for the flu and calls for an even bigger government/private partnership to develop them. To the contrary, a good start at dealing with this mess would be legislation taking government out of either the vaccine development business or the vaccine approval business and giving parents more choice about what is injected into their children.

Part Six

Crony Labor

17

Big Labor Rakes It in: The Auto Bail-out

L IKE THE STIMULUS Act of 2009, the auto bail-out of the same year is by now familiar territory. But there are many aspects of it which are little known and worth recounting.

Why did the George W. Bush administration pour $17.4 billion into rescuing General Motors and Chrysler?[241] Why did the Obama administration then increase the total to $85 billion?[242] The decision was politically unpopular at the time. The idea of taxing school teachers earning $25 an hour or borrowing from China to rescue $60 an hour unionized auto workers did not seem fair, much less economically defensible. Economist Timothy Kehoe, a self-described "lifelong Democrat" and "Obama voter," remarked at the time:" It was scandalous. . . . Unproductive firms need to die. . . ."[243]

The calculus of both administrations was political, not economic. General Motors and Chrysler workers were located primarily in six Midwestern presidential election "swing" states, the states that typically decide the election. In addition, in the case of President Obama, the United Auto Workers Union was a key political ally.

Why were General Motors and Chrysler failing? A principal factor was the uneconomic wages, healthcare plans, and pensions negotiated with the United Auto Workers, which would ironically end up owning the companies along with the US government. Another often overlooked factor was the policies of the US government itself. For example, CAFE laws required that US car manufacturers meet minimum miles per gallon of fuel standards. But the law blocked manufacturers from bringing in the smaller, more fuel efficient cars they made abroad in order to meet the mandated domestic fleet standard. The companies were forced to build small cars in US plants, which they could not do economically because of labor costs. Meanwhile foreign companies manufacturing in the US without unionized employees had no trouble meeting the CAFE rules.[244]

In its auto rescue, the Obama Administration made a deliberate decision to ignore bankruptcy law. General Motors and Chrysler had filed for bankruptcy. The shareholders were already wiped out. Normally assets would have been sold off with proceeds going first to secured lenders (those with specific collateral behind the loan) and then to unsecured creditors of all sorts. The United Auto Workers, as an unsecured creditor, would have gotten little. And in any case, union contracts are usually voided in a bankruptcy proceeding.

The Obama Administration changed all the rules. Consumer warranty contracts from the past were voided,[245] but union contracts were not. Tax losses from the past, usually extinguished in bankruptcy, were carried forward into the new General Motors and Chrysler. This meant that the new companies would not have to pay taxes for many years into the future. The United Auto Workers received a new note for $4.6 billion (45% of its financial claim) against Chrysler and 55% of the company. In the case of General Motors, the union got $10.2 billion in cash (about half its financial claim) and 39% of the company, with the government retaining the rest of the new shares.

Secured creditors of Chrysler and General Motors got about 28% of their money back, much less than they would have received if the union had not received such unprecedented and seemingly illegal special treatment. Why did they not sue? In the first place, many of these creditors were banks that were also being bailed out by the government or under the thumb of its regulators. They were hardly in a position to refuse consent. In the second place, under the "sovereign immunity" doctrine, the government can only be sued when Congress has passed legislation allowing it.

The president also condemned recalcitrant unsecured creditors as "speculators,"[246] and, in the case of some of them, seemed to be threatening regulatory retaliation.

Who were these people? Some of them were Wall Street firms, although often these firms held the bonds on behalf of average Americans. About 20% of all the General Motors bonds were directly owned by "mom-and-pop" investors who had entrusted their retirement savings to a company they thought they could trust. For example, there was David Tuckerman, 84, of Arlington, VA who lost $20,000 of retirement savings; David Talbot, 24, a camp counselor who lost what had been a $5,000 gift from his grandfather; Bill Zastrow, 58, a single father who lost $240,000 in college and retirement savings; and Richard and Willa Woodard, a retired couple who lost most of their retirement savings, $170,000.[247] How could the US government divert money to a major political ally, the union, at the expense of small investors or warranty owners, the people who had trusted GM enough to buy a bond or a car from it?

All of this amounted to what legal scholars call a "sub rosa" reorganization, which is forbidden,[248] as well as a violation of the most fundamental tenets of bankruptcy law. It also violated property rights, some of the most basic rights under Common Law. As commentator Lawrence Kudlow noted, it essentially replaced "the rule of law" with "political decisions."[249]

In addition to the bail-out itself, the federal government supported the new union-owned companies in numerous ways. It spent $17.2 billion rescuing General Motors Acceptance Corp, the financing arm of the company, and spun it out as an independent company under the name Ally, with General Motors retaining 6.7% of the shares.[250] It shifted federal purchase of cars to favor a new electric hybrid, the Volt, made by General Motors, and provided a $7,500 federal tax credit ($2,000 more if you got a more powerful charger) to any consumer buying one. And, very importantly, the US Federal Reserve both directly supported the General Motors and Chrysler finance arms (along with other auto companies' finance arms, including foreign firms[251]) and kept interest rates at vanishing levels, which made car financing much easier.

General Motor's main parts supplier, Delphi, had been in bankruptcy long before the auto makers. President Obama's Auto Task Force handed Delphi over without auction or competitive bidding to a private investment firm affiliated with Platinum Equity, reportedly because Platinum had close ties with the United Auto Workers as well as to the administration.[252] What happened to the pensions of 20,000 non-unionized Delphi workers? Unlike United Auto Workers health plans and pensions, they largely disappeared.[253]

General Motors also had some non-union workers and plants. As the company restructured, it was these plants that were shut down, even the highly productive non-union plant in Moraine, Ohio, a suburb of Dayton. Under terms of the reorganization, workers at this location were barred from transfer to other plants.[254] And as business improved, it was union plants, not non-union, that were opened. The message was clear: a worker foolish enough not to have voted for United Auto Workers' representation had no rights and no future.

The Obama Administration also fired the chief executive of General Motors, named his successor, and took majority ownership of the company. Would General Motors executives now become a reliable source of campaign donations? At first, no. But by 2010, the donations were starting to flow to politicians again, despite the company's new status as a ward of the government.[255]

The donations were already flowing from Evercore Partners, an investment firm that received $64 million in fees for arranging a government bail-out that would have happened anyway. Roger Altman, a former assistant treasury secretary under President Clinton and key Evercore principal, was a close ally of the president and bundler for his campaign. His partner, Ralph Schlosstein, gave a $38,500-a-plate fundraiser for the president and raised $2.1 million for the president and the Democratic National Committee.[256]

At about the same time, the Treasury Department issued a press release stating that "General Motors Repays Treasury Loan in Full."[257] The company's new CEO, Ed Whitacre, restated this in a *Wall Street Journal* article: "We have repaid our government loan, in full, with interest, five years ahead of the original schedule."[258] The message was repeated in a television commercial. But as columnist George Will noted, the claim was "rubbish."[259] The truth was that General Motors had repaid $6.7 billion, and had done so with other funds received from the government, a move that Senator Charles Grassley (R-Iowa) called the "TARP money shuffle."[260]

A little later in 2010, the new General Motors prepared an offering document for a sale of shares to the public. The very last item on a list of "risk factors" was notice that, because the company was majority owned by the government, the offering would be largely exempt from federal and state securities law, including anti-fraud laws. If the prospectus was misleading, as the company's earlier claim of loan repayment was, the buyer would not be able to sue, something completely unprecedented in modern stock offerings.[261]

Another major risk factor for any buyer was the quality of the loans the company was making to sell its cars. Many of the sales were being made to sub-prime borrowers who might or might not be able to make the payments. Within a year, the company's new lending arm, ResCap, had itself filed for bank-ruptcy,[262] the new GM share price had fallen 40%, and *Forbes* was openly wondering if the whole company was headed for another bankruptcy.[263]

Two of the underwriters for the 2010 GM stock issue were identified simply as ICBC and CICC. These were a Chinese state-owned bank and a Chinese partly state-owned investment bank.[264] Evidently the US government, one of the sellers, and the United Auto Workers, another principal seller, hoped to sell shares in China. The United Auto Workers was in fact able to sell a third of its shares, assisted by a promise of the government not to sell any more shares for six months after the initial sale, even though the Union was free to go on selling as it wished.[265]

By 2012, the US government bailed-out General Motors seemed to be particularly focused on China, where sales had been strong. Company executive Dan Akerson said in Beijing that "one of our aims is to help grow a new generation of automotive engineers, designers, and leaders right here in China." The company had already invested $7 billion in China, $1 billion in Mexico, and planned to invest another $1 billion in the kleptocratic economy of Russia.[266]

There was not anything particularly surprising about this. Right at the end of the US presidential campaign in 2012, Chrysler, having been bailed out by the US government but now an Italian company, hinted it might move the production of Jeeps, the prototypically American vehicle, from Ohio to China.[267] The Romney campaign pounced on this and ran an ad about it in Ohio, where one in eight jobs are connected to the auto industry.[268] The ad backfired because Chrysler promptly denied the story and the press claimed it was all a fabrication. The company then gave its employees election day off to be sure they voted for the candidate who had saved their jobs[269]. Not long after came the company announcement that it was indeed thinking of moving some Jeep production to China.

The US government also tried to help General Motors and Chrysler in a variety of other ways. It kept interest rates extremely low, which helped finance car sales. It launched the cash for clunkers program. This involved the government buying about 750,000 old vehicles, which were either incinerated, which was worse for the environment than continuing to run the old cars, or turned into scrap and sold to China. An administration that had stressed its commitment to environmentalism allowed no recycling of parts. The program did increase US car sales, although many of the new sales went to unqualified buyers, which just led directly to repossession. Those whose cars were repossessed found that used cars were now scarce, and much higher in price if available at all. So many people lost their old transportation and were not able to replace it.[270]

By 2013, the Obama administration had reverted to the usual government stance of raising new car prices as well. For example, the Department of Transportation decided to mandate rear-view camera and video displays for all cars, at an estimated cost of $2.7 billion,[271] but delayed the rule for several years. It was put back on the front burner after the 2012 election and was expected to be issued sometime in 2013. This rule might make cars safer. But it would also help to drive the cost of cars beyond the means of low income earners. It would also push low income buyers further into debt or into smaller, cheaper foreign cars.

Some people will no doubt justify the seemingly illegal actions that the US government took to bail out the United Auto workers and its rich store of swing state voters by arguing that unions are on the side of the "little guy" and provide important protections against the selfish actions of predatory corporations. But they should look more closely at what and whom they are supporting. Since the 1930's, union members have generally been more privileged than other workers. For example, the unionized office workers at Southern California ports in 2012 rejected a management offer of $190,000 a year, which included a no layoff provision. They did so even as their strike was tying up US commerce and creating economic losses estimated at $1 billion per day.[272]

It is usually taken for granted that unions raise worker pay and, and by so doing, reduce income inequality and poverty, but none of this is true. Economists have long acknowledged that union wage gains do not come at the expense of owner profits, taken as a whole. They come at the expense of other, non-unionized workers. To see why this is true, we need to realize that unions are government-protected monopolies. That is, they seek to create a monopoly of the labor force for any given industry. Like any monopoly, they may be able to raise the price (in this case of labor) in one industry or industry segment, but as the price rises, employers naturally respond by reducing the numbers hired. The workers not hired because of monopoly prices increase the supply of labor in other industries, which reduces wages there. The result is not an increase in workers' wages overall, just an increase for some and a decrease for others.

Even workers who seem to benefit from the labor monopoly in a given industry may be enjoying illusory gains. The rich wages paid by General Motors and

Chrysler over the years not only led to fewer and fewer hires; it also meant higher and higher car prices. These car prices in turn attracted the foreign competition that eventually destroyed the unionized auto makers. In addition, it meant that US workers had to pay higher prices for their own cars. The result of Detroit union gains in the end was impoverishment for everyone, even the union workers.

18

Public Employee Unions: Crony Capitalism at Its Most Blatant

I N 2006, NEW JERSEY Governor Jon Corzine spoke to a Trenton rally of 10,000 public employees whose pay, benefits, and work rules contract was coming up for negotiation with the state. He promised the assembled throng that "we will fight for a fair contract."[273] This statement was more than a little puzzling. The union would be negotiating with him!

The governor also knew that the union he was "negotiating with" was a prime political backer of his campaigns. Every dollar of wage increases he granted would swell union dues, which workers in New Jersey and 27 other states are forced to pay and which are generally withheld from paychecks by the state. A significant portion of these dues would then come back to the governor in the form of campaign support.

This situation is of course not limited to New Jersey. It has been replayed over and over again in many states, especially those now closest to bankruptcy such as New York, California, and Illinois, all bastions of the Democratic Party, with whom the public unions are closely allied. As Michael Barone has noted, "Public employee unions are a mechanism by which every taxpayer is forced to fund the Democratic Party."[274] This is a bit of an exaggeration. Republican Governor George Pataki (R-New York) made a celebrated deal with the Hospital Workers Union and other labor concessions to win re-election.[275]

Another "special situation" is New York City, where the public unions have launched their own party, the Working Families Party (WFP), originally in conjunction with the now disgraced community organizer, ACORN. WFP usually works with Democrats, but is potentially strong enough to elect its own mayoral candidate. In that case, the unions would not only be negotiating contracts with a political crony; they would be negotiating with themselves.

The New York City Council, like the New York State Senate, has been called "a wholly owned subsidiary of the public sector unions."[276] Former state senator Seymour Lachman has called the political system in the city and state "Boss Tweed's Tammany Hall wrapped in some kind of progressive disguise."[277] This kind of arrangement has not, however, always been a feature of "progressive" politics.

President Woodrow Wilson called a strike by Massachusetts policemen "an intolerable crime against civilization."[278] President Franklin Roosevelt, a close ally of labor unions in general, called the idea of strikes by public workers "unthinkable and intolerable."[279] He added that

> meticulous attention should be paid to the special relations and obligations of public servants to the public itself and to government....[280] [Collective bargaining] cannot be transplanted into the public service. The very nature and purposes of government make it impossible for administrative officials to represent fully or to bind the employer [because] the employer is the whole people, who speak by means of laws.[281]

Roosevelt's major piece of labor legislation, the National Labor Relations Act of 1935, also called the Wagner Act, supported labor unions in numerous ways, and in particular strengthened labor's exemption from anti-trust, an exemption that was sketched out by the Clayton Act of 1914 and became somewhat firmer with the Norris LaGuardia Act of 1932. Without this legislation, it would be illegal for one union to represent all the workers of a single industry. But the Wagner Act pointedly denied federal employees the right to bargain collectively or to strike, and this prohibition remains intact to this day. Even labor leaders agreed with its wisdom. George Meany, longtime president of the largest private union, the AFL-CIO, said that it was "impossible to bargain collectively with the government."²⁸²

Roosevelt's view of the rights and duties of public employees, federal or state, prevailed until 1958. At that time, New York Mayor Robert Wagner, son of the senator whose name was on the 1935 federal bill, granted city workers collective bargaining rights and unions exclusive representation rights. Before long, the city was collecting dues from paychecks, turning them over to the unions, and then relying on the unions to keep Democratic politicians in power through campaign contributions and get-out-the-vote drives.

President Kennedy watched all this from the White House and saw the broader possibilities. In 1962, he signed Executive Order 10988 authorizing and encouraging the unionization of the federal government's workforce, although not the right to bargain collectively or strike. Federal workers had already won numerous legal protections against unreasonable rules; they were almost impossible to fire. So what exactly would the new federal unions such as the American Federation of Government Employees (AFGE) do, other than collect dues and take part in politics? The answer of course was that this was exactly what President Kennedy wanted them to do.

Kennedy's executive order further encouraged the spread of public unions in states and cities. These unions included the American Federation of State, County, and Municipal Employees (AFSCME), the Service Employees International Union (SEIU) (which represents private as well as public employees and has earned a reputation for rough tactics, even including physical threats and intimidation),[283] the American Federation of Teachers (AFT), and National Education Association (NEA). Unlike federal unions, these unions do have collective bargaining rights, do strike, and above all strike terror in the hearts of opposing politicians.

Calvin Coolidge, when Governor of Massachusetts, refused to allow a police strike in 1919, the one President Wilson criticized. This was an act of great courage, since it could have led to public disorder and chaos. Voters agreed and Coolidge was propelled into the vice presidency and then the presidency in 1923. President Ronald Reagan also fired the federal air traffic controllers in 1981, when they illegally went on strike. But these were rare exceptions. As the decades passed, fewer and fewer public officials dared to stand up to labor and to government labor in particular.

Toward the end of the 20th century, private employee labor unions were generally in retreat, while public employee unions were advancing. For example, from 1973 to 2012, union membership in the private sector fell by more than half to 11% and the decline seemed to be accelerating. In contrast, over the same period public unions grew from 23% of the public work-force to 37%.[284]

By 2010, it was estimated that 11 million Americans were forced to join a union, support union political action, and pay union dues, including dues used for political or cultural purposes at odds with their own beliefs, in order to get or keep a job. Total union dues, both private and public, were estimated at $8 billion,[285] a stupendous sum large enough to intimidate almost any politician. No wonder a former president of the California Teachers Association referred to his union as "the fourth, co-equal branch of government. Nobody has [a comparable] political and money war chest."[286]

Of the twenty largest donors in recent federal elections, ten were unions.[287] (These donations were in addition to those of individual public employees, who may also donate on their own.) The three largest public unions gave $171.5 million for the 2010 elections alone,[288] assisted by a Supreme Court decision (Citizens United) in early 2010 that allowed both unions and corporations to spend unlimited amounts on campaigns, so long as their expenditures were "independent," that is, not coordinated with the campaign of the candidate they were supporting. A single union, the SEIU, reported spending $70 million for Democrats during the 2012 presidential election, more even than President Obama's main super PAC, Priorities USA, which spent $54 million.[289]

As more and more money flowed to politicians, especially those on the state and local level, the number of public employees kept rising, to 2.4 million in California alone.[290] And so did their pay, health plans, and retirement plans, along with relaxed disability and retirement rules. It was a kind of Faustian bargain that rolled from state to state, transforming the political landscape as it arrived.

For example, after Democrats won control of both legislative houses in Washington State in 2002, they lifted the public employee collective bargaining restrictions. This led to a doubling of public employee union members in three years. Union spending on Democrats also doubled and enabled Christine Gregoire to become governor in 2004 by 129 votes. The AFSCME union even donated $250,000 to help pay for the recount that sealed her victory.

Gregoire then "negotiated" contracts with the unions providing for large wage increases, some over 25%. Increased union contributions in turn helped Gregoire win re-election in 2008 by 194,614 votes against the same opponent. As J. Vander Stoep, who worked for Gregoire's Republican opponent, noted: "The Democrats . . . are building something, . . . at taxpayer expense, . . . that conceivably can never be undone."[291]

19

Public Sector Union Scandals Begin to Leak

MANY REPORTERS REFLEXIVELY support unions, and prefer not to acknowledge scandals related to them, especially at the local and state level. Nevertheless, troubling news accounts have emerged:

- A New York City sewer engineer is paid $775,000 ($173,000 regular annual rate plus back payments from settlement of a labor dispute).[292]

- A Chicago union leader takes a leave of absence in 1989 from the city's sanitation department, where he earned $40,000, to work for a union. He is then allowed to "retire" from the city at age 56 with $108,000 pension. (The rules say that the individual should waive a union pension to do this. In this case, the official reportedly does not waive the union pension. The city knows this, but grants the city pension anyway.)[293]

■ Another Chicago labor leader is allowed to return to the city payroll for one day in 1994, so that he can then take a formal leave of absence to work for a union. His city pension is $158,000 a year.[294]

■ 16 psychiatrists working for California are paid $400,000 or more. One of them, with a degree from an Afghan medical school, takes home $822,302.[295]

■ A California prison nurse earns $270,000 a year, principally through overtime.[296] Some prison guards earn over $300,000.[297]

■ More than half the lifeguards working for Newport Beach, CA earn more than $150,000 in 2010. One earns $203,481. A lifeguard labor union spokesman comments: "We have negotiated very fair and very reasonable salaries. . . . Lifeguard salaries here are well within the norm of other city employees."[298]

This union spokesman might have also explained that these compensation levels are comparable to those of California legislators, which averaged $140,000 in 2010, excluding extras such as free cars, free gasoline, obscure per diem reimbursements, and even exemptions from traffic tickets or having to pay on toll roads, a perk shared by other state employees as well.[299] Attempts to force California legislators to reveal their total compensation and perks are always left to die in committees so that no one has to record a vote on them.[300]

- In Massachusetts, four state troopers are paid more than $200,000 and 123 over $150,000.[301]

- In New York City, firefighters may retire at half pay after 20 years. The city has 10,000 retired police officers under 50 years old. Pension benefits for a new retiree in 2009 average $73,000, often with a $12,000 year-end bonus, and usually include medical insurance worth $10,000. All is exempt from state and local taxes.[302] Public sector benefits have grown at a rate twice that of the private sector since 2000.

- In New York State, the law requires that any new bill must be evaluated for its effect on the budget. It is revealed that calculations are being made by an actuary who has been fired by the city (note: such firings are notoriously difficult) and whose chief clients are—who else?—the unions. Not surprisingly, he finds little or no budget impact to union benefit increases.[303] Also not surprisingly, New York State has the highest employee pension costs in the country.

- New York lawmakers help the unions in many ways that go beyond directly increasing wages and benefits or relaxing work rules. For example, in 2010 the legis-lature seeks to allow local governments to borrow from the state pension fund in order to meet required payments to the same fund. This is done so that the localities can pretend to be meeting their inflated pension obligations.[304]

- States and localities also help the unions organize more workers and then collect the dues for them. In Michigan, a new union formed by the United Auto Workers and the American Federation of State, County, and Municipal Employees is called the Child Care Providers Together Michigan (CCPTM). There is a problem, however. Since the child care providers targeted by the union work for themselves, who will be the designated employer against whom to organize?

- The new union solves this problem with help from the state of Michigan and the US Department of Health and Human Services. A newly created shell corporation called the Michigan Home Based Child Care Council is granted the right to bargain collectively as a "public employer," even though none of the child care providers works for this entity. In addition, the Michigan Department of Human Services helps out by collecting and remit-ting union dues by withholding a portion of the US government checks provided to low income parents for childcare.

- These checks are paid to the parents, not the child care providers, and are meant to help the low income parent find child care in order to take an outside job. No matter. Some of this money is now siphoned off to the new union. Where does this money go and how is it used? As one child care provider, now enrolled involuntarily in the union, has said, "We have a deduction taken from a check, and where that goes, I have no clue. There's no communication [from the union]." Nor is this Michigan story singular. Fourteen states are facilitating the unionization of child care providers in one way or another.[305]

- In suburban areas of Chicago, some school administrators earn over $400,000 a year.[306] Teachers in the city itself earn an average of $76,000 in wages (before benefits), far more than the average family. Yet the union turns down a contract offering a 4% a year salary increase and goes on strike at the beginning of the fall 2012 school year. A teacher in Michigan says that she "would not recommend to my pupils to become a teacher" because a proposed pension change would prevent her from retiring with pension at age 47.[307]

  Only 15% of fourth graders in the Chicago system are deemed proficient in reading and 44% of high school freshmen do not graduate.[308] Massive teacher contracts not only spell out what the teacher will do every moment of the day; they also make it virtually impossible to fire a teacher. Between 1986 and 2004, a mere 36 of 95,000 public school teachers in Illinois are fired.[309] The result is that education cannot change or improve. Unlike other industries, stagnation is mandated. Some educators and parents try to escape the straightjacket by founding charter schools. But the unions pursue them relentlessly, opposing their founding or insisting, as the DC teachers union has, that charter teachers be forced to join the union and operate under its contract. Steve Jobs, Apple Corp. founder and political "progressive," concluded before his death: "Until the teachers' unions are broken, there is almost no hope for education reform."[310]

The American Federation of Teachers (AFT) collects $211 million in dues in 2010; the National Education Association (NEA) $397 million. With state affiliates included, the total approaches $1 billion. The AFT president makes nearly half a million, and almost 600 officials at the two unions earn over $100,000. $297 million is donated to political campaigns over a decade—with total political spending much higher. It is hard to say how high the spending really is because members do not receive complete information.[311]

■ Not all unionized school employees are teachers, of course, and this creates its own set of demands.

For example, the Chicago school system does not allow kids to bring lunches from home, unless they have a note from a doctor. Why? Is it because school lunches are so nutritious that no kid should miss them? No. The school lunch program of the federal government is a nest of crony capitalism, with a pizza classified as a vegetable to please the pizza makers, and meat irradiated to ensure that the unsold Iowa beef dumped at Iowa Senator Harkin's insistence is not putrid.

No, the reason for the Chicago rules is different. If students could bring their own food, there would be fewer jobs for the school lunch employees affiliated with the super-powerful Service Employees International Union. The union wants more of these employees, not fewer, and also insists on benefits and wages that in many cases are further bankrupting the schools.[312]

The same union also wants more and more sick days for its workers (just for the protection of the children it says), plus more dinners and summer meals for children. Naturally First Lady Michelle Obama is working closely with the union as she promotes an expanded school lunch program.[313] Meanwhile 35% of the Chicago school cafeterias have failed at least one city health department inspection. In one case, the staff had to be replaced, which was no easy administrative feat, before the school finally got a clean bill of health.[314]

- North Carolina does allow home packed lunches, but preschooler's lunches must be checked and approved by school authorities. In one instance, a lunch consisting of a turkey and cheese sandwich, a banana, apple juice, and chips is rejected and the child is given cafeteria chicken nuggets instead.[315]

- In 2012, a bipartisan task force, co-chaired by respected New York Democrat Richard Ravitch and former Federal Reserve Chairman Paul Volcker, takes a close look at Illinois's state finances. Commenting on their work, *New York Times* reporter Mary Williams Walsh notes that

  > Illinois has the lowest credit rating of the 50 states and has America's second-biggest public debt per capita, $9,624, including state and local borrowing. Only New York State's debt is bigger at $13,840 per capita. But Illinois has not been able to use much of the borrowed money to keep its roads, bridges, and schools in good working order.

  > Nearly two-thirds of the Illinois state government's $58 billion in direct debt consists of bonds the government issued to cover retirement payments for workers....

  > Yet despite all that borrowing, Illinois's public pension system is still in tatters. In

fact, its total pension shortfall is conserva-
tively estimated at $85 billion. . . . The task
force said that further reductions in pension benefits appear inevitable, though legally difficult.[316]

Commentator Walter Russell Mead says about
this:

Illinois politicians, including the present president of the United States, have
wrecked one of the country's potentially
most prosperous and dynamic states, condemned millions of poor children to substandard education, failed to maintain
vital infrastructure, choked business development and growth through unsustainable tax and regulatory policies—and
still failed to appease the demands of the
public sector unions and fee-seeking Wall
Street crony capitalists who make billions
off the state's distress.

Blue [state] politicians speak eloquently
and often sincerely about their desire to
help the poor. They speak beautifully about
the need for better schools. . . . But these
beautiful sentiments have less and less to
do with the actual policies they pursue.[317]

- For the fifty states as a whole, unfunded public employee benefit liabilities are at least $1.26 trillion, according to the PEW Center on the states.[318]

- As financial pressures mount on states and localities, some try to escape the union chokehold by hiring part-time workers, by giving workers "contractor" rather than "employee status" to avoid benefits, and by paying minimum wages to the new hires. In this way, the union system creates two classes of employees, one favored and one far less favored.[319] One municipality, Camden, New Jersey, choked in crime and unable to pay the large sums demanded by the police union, responded by disbanding its entire 230 member police force and asking the county to provide a new 400 member force at lower wages.[320]

In all these moves, there is a great deal of uncertainty. Can governments, for example, revise retirement benefit provisions of contracts? The unions say no. Famed attorney David Boies, in a Rhode Island test case, says yes: "There is no contract. Even if there was a contract, the state, pursuing the public interest, has the right to modify contracts."[321] Time and courts will decide who is right.

20

Public Union Foes
and Defenders

THE BASIC PREMISE behind public employee-financed campaigns is that the election is now while the bills may be deferred for years, particularly if they take the form of pension promises. Eventually, however, the bills do come due. This is why Governor Mitch Daniels (R-Indiana) said he decided on his first day of office in 2005[322] to end public employee collective bargaining rights and to stop collecting union dues. Without the state collecting dues, only 10% of union members chose to stay enrolled by paying their own dues.[323]

Governor Chris Christie (R-New Jersey) stood before 200 of his state's mayors in 2010 and declared that the era of "Alice-in-Wonderland" budgeting is over: "Money does not grow on trees. . . . For New Jersey and any number of other states and municipalities, it's useless to pretend. . . . We have no room left to borrow. We have no room left to tax."[324] Chris Christie went on to say that his treasurer had presented him with 378 possible budget deletions or freezes to balance the budget and that he had adopted 375. Almost all observers thought that this was the end of the Governor's career. Instead it made him a national figure and even won approval from New Jersey voters.

Governor Scott Walker (R-Wisconsin) was elected in 2010 and immediately moved to restrict collective bargaining for benefits (excluding police and fire) and also to stop collecting union dues. This led to a firestorm of protest and a recall election, which the Governor won. Governor John Kasich (R-Ohio), also elected in 2010, restricted public employee collective bargaining, including police and fire, but his actions were overturned by voters in a 2011 referendum.

In retrospect, Kasich's chief error was in not moving to end automatic state collection of all union dues. Scott Walker's experience in Wisconsin in this regard is highly instructive. Walker's position was that the state would continue collecting all dues until the end of the contract. After that, dues would only be collected with the consent of the public worker. What actually happened was that two-thirds of workers enrolled in AFSCME, the state's largest public union apart from the teachers' NEA, refused to give their consent. As in Indiana, the political power of the union took a major hit. As Jim Geraghty commented in the *National Review*: "Apply this across the country . . . and you're talking about . . . a game-changer in so many states."[325]

Ironically, a federal court ruled in 1966 that a union did not have the right to use member dues for political purposes if a member objects. But few union members know about the right to opt out or, if they do, may feel intimidated in pursuing what are called their "Beck rights." Moreover the unions make it very difficult by stalling on Beck rights requests, smothering them in endless red tape, and refusing to calculate what portion of the dues apply. If, however, the public employer refuses to collect full dues for the union automatically and instead asks the member whether dues should be used for political purposes, it is much easier for the worker to express a preference.[326]

As we have noted, the rules governing state and local public unions differ from those governing federal workers. The former can usually engage in collective bargaining and go on strike; the latter seem to serve little purpose other than to collect dues and put a share of it at the disposal of the Democratic Party. Despite these differences, federal wages and benefits have also risen, so that taken together they now exceed what can be earned in the private sector for the same job. This is a remarkable reversal: fifty years ago, it was generally understood that federal workers would earn less in exchange for more days off, slightly better benefits, and almost total job security.

Studies purporting to compare federal with private work levels do not agree with one another, but the Congressional Budget Office has found that, comparing employees of comparable educational level, federal wages are higher at lower pay scales, similar at middle, and somewhat lower at the high end, with benefits much higher across the board.[327] Taken together, the federal employee advantage is 16%. In addition, federal employees work three hours less per week on average and one month less per year.[328] An earlier Labor Department study found that state and local workers make 46% more,[329] so federal workers were not doing as well. Other studies, however, suggest all categories of government pay are more like twice as high as private, when the net present value of soaring retirement awards, often equal to final year pay, is taken into account.[330]

The number of very highly paid federal employees has also increased, even during the years following the Crash of 2008. For example, in early 2008, the Labor Department had only one employee earning $170,000 or more. Eighteen months later, there were 1,690 such employees.[331] Over the same period, all federal employees making more than $100,000 rose from 14% to 19%.[332] One federal employee, working in a government green energy lab in Colorado, was reported in 2012 to be making just under $1 million, with two deputies making over $500,000 each, and nine others making over $350,000.[333] The number of all jobs during the economic recession of 2008–2009 also rose in the federal government, unlike in the private sector, where over eight million disappeared.[334] It is not at all surprising that by the end of 2010, seven of the ten richest counties in the US surrounded Washington, DC.[335]

Having come into office on a wave of union support and money, the Obama administration literally opened its doors to union leaders. Andy Stern, the head of the powerful SEIU, visited the White House more often than any other political figure during the first six months.[336] What he seemed to want most was "Card Check" legislation that would end the secret ballot in union organizing. President Obama and Democratic leaders strongly endorsed the bill, but it must have lacked some Democratic votes in the Senate, because it was never put forward for a vote, despite overwhelming Democratic majorities in Congress.

President Obama found other ways to reward labor. During his first weeks in office, he signed executive order 13502, which made union membership a requirement of anyone working on federal construction projects.[337] He also opposed Senator Jim DeMint's (R-South Carolina) National Right to Work bill, which would have ended compulsory union membership as a job condition in all states (23 states have their own versions of this law).

The President backed a decision by the Democrat controlled National Labor Relations Board (NLRB) intended to block Boeing's plan to move 787 Dreamliner plane construction from unionized Washington to union-free South Carolina.[338] He backed another highly controversial decision to force companies to turn over their employees' private email addresses and telephone numbers without employee consent to union organizers.[339] He also tried unsuccessfully to force companies doing business with the government to reveal all political activity or donations, a rule that would not have applied to unions.[340] By early 2012, he had granted waivers from his Obamacare legislation to unions representing 543,812 employees (also to administration friendly companies with 69,813 employees).[341]

Meanwhile the president kept subsidies flowing to the Post Office which, despite massive losses, reliably collects union dues from workers, which are then made available to Democratic campaigns ($3.6 million in the 2010 election cycle).[342] Other countries have successfully privatized their mail delivery. The obstacle to doing this in the US is that postal workers, like other government employees, are deemed to be, for the most part, reliable Democratic voters, and their union is regarded as an indispensable political cash cow.

21

Not All State and Local Cronyism Involves Unions

A N EARLIER CHAPTER described how Valerie Jarrett, best known as President Obama's most intimate White House Advisor, turned a job in the Chicago mayor's office into a personal real estate holding worth as much as $5 million. This is not unusual. Big real estate deals in major American cities are the mother's milk of politics. Developers get rich from special tax and other deals, politicians get campaign contributions, and former politicians or former aides charge for access.

Here is one way it is done:

Step 1: Collect property taxes in a "redevelop-
ment" agency.

Step 2: Use these funds to subsidize favored developers or businesses.

Step 3: Or use these funds to build major projects
which favored developers or businesses can
buy at deep discounts.

Step 4: Waive property taxes.

Step 5: In some cases, promise payments to a new
business coming in equal to whatever their
employees pay in state or local taxes.[343]

All this and more has happened in Los Angeles. No
wonder local retail developer Jose de Jesus Legaspi
says "It's extremely difficult to do business in Los
Angeles.... Everyone has to kiss the rings of the [City
Hall politicians.]"[344]

Sometimes, like Valerie Jarrett, the political dons
do not wait to leave office before enriching themselves
personally. And sometimes this is not done with any
subtlety. In the town of Bell, CA, the city manager was
caught paying himself $1.5 million (salary and benefits)
a year, with a $600,000-a-year pension obligation. An
assistant manager was paid $845,960, the police chief
$700,000 (while laying off police), and city council-
men $100,000 for part-time "work." After all this came
to light, the top three offenders were forced out and
the city councilmen cut to $10,000.[345]

To emphasize the point that not all state and local cronyism involves unions, one need only look at union-unfriendly Texas. Here is what Dave Nalle, secretary of the in-state Republican Liberty Caucus, says about Republican Governor Rick Perry:

> Perry . . . loves to use taxpayer money to subsidize his business cronies. . . . His supposed belief in limited government and in states' rights conveniently disappears whenever it conflicts with the demands of the special interests and corporate cronies he serves.[346]

Nalle also recounts how Perry set up the Texas Enterprise Fund and Texas Emerging Growth Fund which enabled him to pour at least $43 million of the $700 million funds into alleged crony businesses.[347]

We have already described in an earlier chapter how Perry mandated a dangerous vaccine for teenage girls while taking money from the vaccine's manufacturer. When FEMA and other federal disaster funds became available after Hurricane Katrina, Perry allegedly tried to divert them to his allies. The Obama administration objected, but a "deal" was struck on $3.2 billion of allocations.[348] The Governor's wife, Anita, has worked as a fundraiser for the Texas Association Against Sexual Assault. This group receives donations from state agencies, including the governor's office, as well as from Perry political donors.[349]

Although much of the cronyism at the state and local level involves unions, developers, or other business interests, nonprofits are often part of the action. The Academy of Nutrition and Dietetics, formerly the American Dietetic Association, has been trying for years to set up state licensing boards that would, in effect, create a nutritional counseling monopoly for its members. The organization already has a monopoly on Medicare reimbursement, achieved by careful cultivation of federal contacts over the years, and monopolies on advising hospitals, prisons, and schools on food programs. The nutritional value, much less the taste of most hospital and school food, run by AND members, speaks for itself. In addition, AND members need only hold a college degree, so that the effect of AND's restrictive state licensing efforts is often paradoxically to exclude nutritionists with masters and PhD degrees.[350]

The theme of eliminating or trying to eliminate competition through deals with state or local legislators is a familiar one. In New Jersey, when the president of the Liquor Store Alliance was asked why state law does not allow microbrew pubs, he replied that he didn't mind giving the microbrews a few breaks, but "what we don't want to do is become competitors with one another."[351]

In addition, in Louisiana, a state funerals board (eight of whose nine members were from industry) ruled that the monks of St. Joseph Abbey in Covington could not continue to make simple, handmade pine and cypress caskets.[352] In Nashville, Tennessee, taxi companies persuaded the city to require a minimum $45 charge for any limo ride, to regulate the age of any limo used, and to forbid cell phone dispatching, which is what new limo companies or drivers do.[353] In Chicago and Washington, DC, the use of a cell phone app by a new service named Uber set the taxicab commission to fuming and the established companies to suing. The DC City Council proposed an amendment that would have legalized Uber, but only if the minimum charge was five times the average taxi cab fare.[354]

The purpose of all these laws is to limit competition, restrict the number of competitors, bar new entrants, and thus protect established companies with ties to politicians. In Virginia, interior designers are required to get a four-year design degree, intern with a licensed designer for two more years, and pass an exam before applying for the certification needed to work.[355] Hairdressers in most states have to jump through numerous such hoops. Sometimes local authorities have an additional motive: to collect fees or taxes. Philadelphia has sent out notices to local internet bloggers informing them that they owe a $300 city business license fee.[356]

In this atmosphere, the only certain growth industry seems to be political lobbying. Everyone needs a lobbyist. Even governments need lobbyists, since local governments must troll for deals with the state government and both local and state governments must troll for deals with Washington. For the decade ending 2010, local and state governments reportedly spent $1.2 billion on federal lobbying. There were 13,000 registered lobbyists working in Washington, but the total number of people seeking to influence legislation is far greater.[357]

Part Seven

Crony Lawyers

22

Legal Predators

JUST AS THE military is supposed to protect us from invasion and the police from criminals, lawyers are supposed to protect us from predatory misuse of civil or criminal law or from legal injustice. Because of their quasi-official role, they have historically regarded themselves rather like doctors, members of a "helping" profession bound to a demanding code of ethics.

Until 1977, lawyers could not legally advertise. They could set themselves up as partnerships but not corporations. If a lawyer built up a huge firm from scratch, he was not able to sell his interest or otherwise profit from it after retirement. The law was supposed to be a calling, not a business.

There are still vestiges of the old legal ethics, but much of it is gone. Most lawyers now regard law as a business. If so it is not your run-of-the-mill business. When it is profit maximizing, it is often feeding parasitically off other successful businesses. In addition to the traditional services—drawing up wills, contracts, court defense—some lawyers are now engaged in what might be described as legal "shakedowns," or in providing "protection" services against such "shakedowns." Moreover, there are so many laws now, and they are often so vague or unintelligible, that almost anyone might need "protection"—if not against predatory lawyers, then against ambitious "on-the-make" public prosecutors.

If lawyers become predators themselves in addition to protectors, that puts all of us at risk. If predatory lawyers form alliances with public officials, that is even more dangerous. If in some instances courts collude with them, that destroys the very fabric of a society. Examples follow.

1. Asbestos

Some of the most useful work on what he calls Trial Lawyers, Inc. has been done by James R. Copland of the Manhattan Institute. Copland writes about asbestos:

> Much of modern asbestos litigation has involved the filing of lawsuits by individuals who aren't sick [from exposure to the product] against companies that never

made the product. . . . As recently noted by Chief Judge Dennis Jacobs of the Second Circuit US Court of Appeals, judges in asbestos litigation have all too often processed massive caseloads "without regard to whether the claims themselves are based on fraud, corrupt experts, [and] perjury." . . . A Pennsylvania judge was convicted of soliciting bribes from attorneys with asbestos dockets before him.[358]

Famed asbestos attorney Dickie Scruggs of Mississippi was jailed for attempting to bribe a judge, although not in an asbestos case. The case in question involved a claim by another law firm for $26.5 million of fees from successful suits of insurers after Hurricane Katrina. Scruggs, also a veteran of tobacco and other liability cases, allegedly the richest man in Mississippi, celebrated for his airplanes, yachts, and lavish lifestyle, brother-in-law of a US senator, offered a state judge $40,000 to rule for him.

2. Healthcare

The Manhattan Institute says about healthcare litigation:

The insurance firm Tillinghast Towers-Perrin places[s] the total direct cost of medical-malpractice litigation at $30.4 billion annually—an expense that has grown almost twice as fast as overall tort litigation and over four times as fast a healthcare inflation 1975–[2008]. . . .[359] A . . . Harvard Medical Practice Group study . . . found that the vast majority of medical-malpractice suits did not involve actual medical injury—and that most cases in which there was actual injury involved no doctor error. . . . [360]

A . . . survey published in the *Journal of the American Medical Association* [revealed that] 93 per cent of doctors said they . . . practiced defensive medicine [because of the threat of lawsuit]. . . .[361] PriceWaterhouseCoopers estimated that 10% of all health-care spending is consumed by medical-malpractice-liability-related defensive medicine and insurance costs—a total sum of $210 billion a year.[362]

Former senator, presidential candidate, and vice presidential nominee John Edwards (D-North Carolina) amassed a personal fortune estimated by *Money Magazine* in 2007 at $55 million as a trial lawyer specializing in medical malpractice, especially childbirth. He won awards of as much as $6.5 million by arguing that children born with cerebral palsy were damaged by the delivery, although most experts believe this condition already exists before delivery. A sharp increase in C-section births, thought to be driven by lawsuit fears, has not reduced its incidence, which supports the idea that it is not associated with delivery.[363]

It is not known how much of his awards Edwards shared with his clients, but the industry standard is 50% or less. Asbestos plaintiffs have received an estimated 42%, with the rest going to "expenses" and lawyer's fees.[364] When lawyers receive more than plaintiffs, there is both money and incentive to file ever more suits.

It is not, of course, easy to know exactly why defensive medicine is being practiced. For example, an *Archives of Internal Medicine* study found that many more colonoscopies for older people were performed, and billed to Medicare, than were indicated by professional guidelines.[365] This might have been for lawsuit avoidance reasons. But it could also have been because the procedure, however uncomfortable and even dangerous for an elderly patient, is expensive and profitable. It is, in effect, a thriving medical industry, and because it is so-called preventive medicine, abuses are almost impossible to spot.

As big as the malpractice awards can be, they are still dwarfed by class action judgments against drug companies. According to the Manhattan Institute, Wyeth's (now Pfizer's) reserve for Fen-Phen litigation in 2005 was $21 billion and Merck's for Vioxx $50 billion. Drug liability is a particularly complicated subject. The cost of Food and Drug Administration approval for a new drug ($1 billion on average) is so high that there is enormous pressure on all parties to do what is necessary to get the product through. Any failure of disclosure or procedure, however, can lead to gigantic judgments, and some of that judgment is likely to find its way back to politicians in the form of campaign contributions. This creates a dilemma for drug companies. On the one hand, they are granted invaluable monopoly rights by the government in the form of patents and FDA approval. But, on the other hand, if they fail adequately to "feed" the politicians, and thus protect themselves, the trial lawyers may eventually claim more and more of the profits.

3. Alliances with State Attorneys General

Forty-three of 50 states elect the Attorney General. Trial lawyers are often major donors to the Attorney General's campaign. In 40 states, the Attorney General may then hire the campaign donor to represent the state with a lucrative contingency fee on an important case. Examples follow.

a. Tobacco

In the mid-1990s, the Texas Attorney General's office had an annual budget of $271 million and employed

600 lawyers. Nevertheless, when private trial lawyers proposed a state Medicaid lawsuit against tobacco companies, they were hired to run it on a contingency fee basis, and never mind that they had contributed $150,000 to the Attorney General's, Dan Morales's, campaigns. When the tobacco companies settled, thereby eliminating any trial work, these lawyers claimed $2.3 billion, which on arbitration was not reduced, but rather increased to $3.3 billion, all money that could have and should have gone to the state of Texas.[366]

In Mississippi, Attorney General Mike Moore chose his largest campaign donor, Richard Scruggs (the same one who later went to jail for bribery) to lead that state's Medicaid suit against the tobacco companies. Arbitrators decided that Scruggs's firm could take $1.4 billion, or 35%, of the $4 billion settlement.[367]

In Florida, an arbitration panel ignored a judge's instruction to reduce the outside counsel's contingency fee of $2.8 billion and instead increased it by an extra $600 million. It has been estimated that this was equivalent to $112,000 per hour of work.[368]

And why did tobacco companies agree in 1998 to an overall settlement with states costing an estimated $246 billion? Why did they choose to forego the right to trial, when they arguably had a good case, because it is difficult to prove that smoking is the direct cause of most illnesses or that smokers should not be held responsible for their own behavior. The most likely reason they settled is that the states not only promised to protect them against any more claims if they did so; they also promised in effect to grant state-supported monopoly status to the tobacco companies involved. After the settlement, the states had a big stake in protecting the tobacco companies, and with that protection it was easy to raise prices sufficiently to cover all the settlement costs.

In reviewing this, we should also keep in mind who smokers are. They are overwhelmingly poor compared to the rest of the population. Consequently, when states protect major tobacco companies, enable their price increases, lay on additional taxes, and simultaneously outlaw the sale of loose tobacco in conjunction with cigarette paper rolling machines, a low cost and probably healthier alternative, they are mainly striking at the most disadvantaged members of society.

b. State Pension Funds

Whenever the price of a publicly traded stock falls sharply, some trial lawyer is likely to become interested. Will it be possible to charge the company with incomplete financial disclosure, perhaps even fraud? An abusive way to explore this is to claim that a nonexistent and anonymous tipster has provided information, then sue and hope that the "discovery process" (in which the defendant must produce documents, especially emails) will produce some "dirt."

To get a lawsuit rolling, the lawyer needs a client, and what better client than a state or other public pension fund, if you have been donating to the Attorney General or another official in charge of the fund? It also helps if you have established good relations with the fund trustees. This is presumably why the class action law firm Bernstein, Litowitz, Berger, and Grossman invited several hundred guests, including teachers, police, and firefighters, to a three-day "conference" in New York City featuring talks by celebrities, special dinners, and a Broadway show. *Forbes* magazine, reporting on this, noted that securities class action suits had pulled in $3.1 billion in 2008, and were likely to increase, thanks to the Crash of that year.[369]

New York comptroller Alan Hevesi chose the law firm of Milberg Weiss to represent the state's common pension fund in securities class actions, a firm that had donated $100,000 to him for the 2002 campaign.[370] Bill Lerach and Mel Weiss of that firm were later convicted of illegal payments to plaintiffs of $11 million over two decades and sentenced to 24 and 30 months in prison. Hevesi was also convicted in 2011 and sentenced to 1-4 years in jail, but for a different crime: steering $250 million in pension assets to an investment firm for $1 million of benefits including campaign donations.[371]

4. California's Prop 65

It is not uncommon for California office buildings to put up a sign near the entrance: "Prop 65 notice— there may be carcinogenics in this building harmful to pregnant women. . . ." The reason for the sign is to forestall a suit under Proposition 65, an initiative passed by California voters in 1986 that is formally known as the Safe Drinking Water and Toxic Enforcement Act.

This notorious act requires that buildings and consumer products, including dietary supplements, post a warning notice if any of (now) 775 chemicals are present in "toxic" amounts. If notice is not posted, anyone can file a complaint. If the Attorney General chooses to sue, the state will collect damages. Otherwise, the original complainant may sue and collect a substantial financial award.

Whatever the original intentions of Prop 65, it has become a means for lawyers to blackmail consumer companies, especially supplement producers. How can they test for 775 different chemicals? In most cases, California has not even set a tolerable limit, and when a limit has been set, it is often unrealistically low.

For example, one serving of spinach typically contains 8.5 mcg of lead. This is not a health hazard. The human body easily eliminates a reasonable amount of lead from the diet each day and spinach is rightly considered a health food. But the Prop 65 limit for pregnant and nursing women is 0.5 mcg. Paradoxically, the more natural the supplement, the more its ingredients are made from safe, wholesome food, the more likely it is to be scored as "toxic" in a Prop 65 lawsuit.

As previously noted, lawyers need to represent a client, so they make a deal with a consumer. Complaints are then filed in the consumer's name, with the same name used over and over again. The object is to wring money out of the defendant without having to do much work, so an offer of settlement is made that is well below the cost of mounting a trial defense. This strategy is usually effective, and an estimated $142 million was paid out in Prop 65 settlements between 2000 and 2010. When legitimate law firms are hired to defend against the Prop 65 legal "bucket shops," they may like the settlements too. Keeping the predators in business means more legal fees for everyone.[372]

5. Bribery Law

A *Forbes* magazine headline from 2010 reads: "The Bribery Law Racket: Bad Guys Abroad Extort Money From a Corporation. Back Home, a Bigger Extortion Awaits." The article under the headline relates how a company that discovers or suspects payment of a bribe by an overseas employee is required to report this to the Justice Department. The company then hires expensive lawyers and accountants to investigate further (with results reported to Justice), pays federal fines, and hires government mandated monitors, often expensive lawyers who have previously worked in government and know the federal regulators.

All of this can be a bottomless pit, costing in some cases hundreds of millions of dollars, and often involving the Securities and Exchange Commission (SEC) as well. Joseph Covington, who headed the Justice Department's Foreign Corrupt Practices Act division in the 1980s, told *Forbes*: "This is good business for [many parties including] Justice Department lawyers who create the marketplace and then get . . . a job [there]."[373] This particular pattern is not limited to foreign bribery cases. If a company gets in trouble with the Federal Trade Commission (FTC) or Food and Drug Administration (FDA) and agrees to a "settlement," the terms may include ongoing "monitoring" by highly paid lawyers, who may just happen to be former FTC or FDA employees.

6. The Brave New World of Court Approved Product Performance Standards

In the spring of 2012, Ohio's 6th Circuit federal court accepted a class action suit named Glazer vs. Whirlpool. Two Ohio residents claimed that their front-loading washing machines produced an offensive odor, though not a medically harmful odor, and on this basis, the court allowed plaintiffs to represent all Ohio purchasers of washers from any manufacturer since 2001. The court did not even rely on Ohio law, as it should have, but imported some California law with no applicability in Ohio in order to suggest that buyers might have been harmed by paying a high price for what might have been an under-performing product.

If ever there was an Alice-in-Wonderland case, this was it. But it had immense implications. If it succeeded, in effect the courts would put themselves in charge of deciding the product specifications and performance standards of all industrial goods. And every manufacturer would have to build these potential litigation costs into the product's price.

In a market system, consumers are supposed to judge products and to vote with their dollars. Overpriced or substandard goods will be rejected and producers suffer the consequences. But if the 6th circuit reasoning prevails, this market system will be short circuited by legal claims based on no demonstrated injury. Millions of consumers will be swept into specious cases as plaintiffs with or without their consent.[374]

23

The Trial Lawyer
Money Machine

IT IS CLEAR enough how government lawyers can exploit the system by creating opaque legal holes, from which companies can never quite climb out, and then enter private practice to "help" them out. These lawyers are profiting both from what they know and whom they know. But how do lawyers who have never worked in government, including disgraced lawyers such as Richard Scruggs or Bill Lerach, get access to government officials? The answer is that they seem to buy it.

For the decade ending 2009, lawyers donated $725 million for state political campaigns and $780 million for federal campaigns.[375] This was far more than any other industry. In addition, lawyers' contributions are more concentrated.

It is not that their contributions always go to Democrats. The Beasley Allen firm gave $240,000 to support Alabama Republican Attorney General Troy King's campaign, and was hired by King to sue drug companies over Medicaid payments, resulting in millions of dollars of revenue for the firm. The Steele and Biggs firm gave $58,000 to Utah Republican Attorney General Mark Shurtleff's campaign, and was hired by the state to sue Eli Lilly over the drug Zyprexa, resulting in $4 million in revenue.[376] But, especially on the national level, lawyers favor Democrats over Republicans by an even higher percentage than labor unions.[377]

As of 2010, both top donors to Senate Majority Whip Dick Durbin (R–Illinois) and four of the top seven donors to Senate Majority Leader Harry Reid (D-Nevada) were plaintiff bar firms. No wonder the late asbestos lawyer, Fred Baron, reacted to a *Wall Street Journal* article charging that the plaintiff's bar "all but ran the Senate," by responding that he strongly disagreed with the "all but."[378]

The American Association for Justice (formerly the American Association of Trial Lawyers of America) donated $2.6 million to federal candidates in 2009–2010. 97% of this went to Democrats.[379] In the 2008 electoral cycle, the AAJ was the second largest single contributor to the Democrats at $2.6 million, only exceeded by the $3.3 million donated by the International Brotherhood of Electrical Workers.[380]

There have been attempts (by Republicans of course) to rein in the trial lawyers. George W. Bush, newly elected governor of Texas in 1995, called a special session of the legislature to take up a tort reform bill that would cap punitive damages, restrict class actions to federal court, and penalize frivolous suits. This bill was approved in Texas and a similar one was approved in Mississippi. In 2001, President Bush successfully passed a bill protecting teachers from civil suit. The trial lawyers put up a fight, but were thwarted because Bush had teachers—another key Democratic donor base—on his side. By cleverly splitting the Democratic coalition, the bill was virtually ensured passage.[381]

Although the Bush administration won some skirmishes with the trial bar, it failed to draw blood. When the Democrats captured the presidency along with large House and Senate majorities in 2008, the tables were turned. Bills were introduced in Congress to:

- Forbid arbitration in nursing home disputes;

- Gut arbitration contracts in general;

- Strip FDA approved medical devices of liability protections;

- Extend suit against corporations accused of fraud to other corporations that had done business with the accused;

- Create more favorable tax treatment of legal expenses on contingency cases (a benefit estimated to be worth $1.6 billion);

- Enable state juries to override federal regulations;

- Reverse a Supreme Court ruling against suits filed with no factual basis (just a hope to find one through "discovery");

- Authorize the unemployed to sue employers for discrimination (an Obama legislative initiative in the "Jobs Act," that was primarily intended as a gift to the trial lawyers, and seemingly overlooked by the media);

- And give employees more years in which to sue over discrimination.[382]

Most of these legislative initiatives ultimately failed, although they put politicians on notice about the power of the trial bar. The last initiative, giving employees more years in which to sue against discrimination, did pass. It was called the Lillie Ledbetter Fair Pay Act of 2009 and promoted as a women's rights bill rather than a trial lawyer's bill. President Obama cited it often during the 2012 presidential campaign without of course ever mentioning the connection to trial lawyers.

Of the 15 million wrongful personal injury tort cases a year in the United States, the vast majority are filed in a relatively few states. Accordingly, while there are 80 lawyers per 10,000 population in New York (far higher in Manhattan alone), there are only 20 in South Carolina and Arizona. Fewer than 1% of these cases come to trial, probably because they cost so much. One side usually runs out of money or decides that it is not worth proceeding. As we have seen, however, with Prop 65 in California, the object of lawyers filing suit is often to avoid the work and expense of a trial. They just want to be paid to drop the suit. When paid off, as they often are, especially if their demands are not excessive, they are both funded and encouraged to file more shakedown suits.

The website Commongood.org, which draws on the work of Philip K. Howard, notes that the US Code now contains 47,000 pages of statutes (laws), The Code of Federal Regulations is even longer at 160,000 pages, and this does not even consider state and local laws and regulations.[383] In many cases, the laws are vague, sometimes intentionally so. The language is impenetrable except by experts, again sometimes intentionally so, to make opposition harder. The regulations are intrusive, as if the government can write a how-to-manual for commerce or everyday life.

Common Good proposes that no law be allowed to be over 50 pages, which would be 34 pages longer than the US Constitution. Legislation should have "sunset" provisions so that laws do not persist forever, one piled atop another, strangling society, but are periodically revised, replaced, or allowed to die. Another good reform would be to require regulations to be reviewed and specifically voted on by legislators, with laws not effective until this is done. In addition, many codes, especially tax codes, should be massively simplified. It is well understood that the tax code, like other codes, is so complex because this permits payoffs to one set of special interests, along with donations aimed at preventing such payoffs from another set of special interests.

It is impossible to calculate the unnecessary cost imposed on the American economy by suffocating laws, compliance, and vigilance against frivolous or unfair lawsuits. These costs are especially burdensome for small businesses, including new businesses, which are by definition small. In the 19th and early 20th century, the ultimate American dream was to invent something new and get a patent on it. Today it costs a fortune to get a patent. And you'll need not just one, but many global patents. Once you have them, they must be defended against the lawsuits of large companies, suits specifically intended to bankrupt the new competitor. The new entrant must prove that the large companies are infringing on the new patents, a very expensive process apart from the legal fees. The ultimate loser is the American public, because small and especially new businesses are the largest source of new jobs.

Part Eight

Beyond the Usual Suspects

24

Reaching Out Globally

A T THE VERY heart of US crony capitalism lies a financial arrangement with China. The US imports Chinese goods, paying with dollars. The Chinese exporters deliver the dollars to the Chinese government which exchanges them for newly printed Renminbi (RMB or Yuan). The government then buys, or often buys, US government bonds, thereby returning the dollars to the US. Thus, in effect, the Chinese finance the purchase of their own goods. If they did not, the dollar would likely fall too low for the Americans to keep buying.

This is a classic maneuver, well understood from the history of mercantilism, a 16th and 17th century form of global crony capitalism. Like other crony capitalist maneuvers, it is convenient for the governments involved, but ultimately unsustainable. Sellers need real buyers, not buyers who are paid to buy.

For this and other reasons, the Chinese government is ambivalent about its relations with the US. On the one hand, it chooses to placate its military by projecting more and more military power against the US. On the other hand, it wants the US to go on borrowing and spending to keep its factories humming. As a further complication, it worries that the printing of so much Chinese currency threatens domestic inflation. And it worries about the value of the US bonds piling up at the Chinese central bank. The United States has a reserve currency, which gives it the unique right to pay its debts in dollars, and nothing really prevents the US from printing more and more dollars until they are worthless. In that event, the Chinese would have sold their goods for nothing.

The Chinese are not of course alone in selling to the US on credit. So do the Japanese and others. At least the Japanese believe that they are getting military protection as part of the bargain.

All of these crony capitalist maneuvers and distortions give today's world governments plenty to worry about. (Will it all blow up on our watch?) But there are also minor deals to be made and abused. For example, the United Nations set up a Clean Development Mechanism designed to encourage a shift away from

the use of chlorofluorocarbons (CFCs) as refrigera-
tor and other coolants, because these chemicals were
destroying the earth's ozone layer. The substitute
chemical, HCFC-22, unfortunately had a drawback.
It produces a byproduct, HFC-23, which is a greenhouse gas, 11,700 times more powerful as a climate-
warming gas than carbon dioxide. When the United
Nations began paying to destroy HFC-23, that just
persuaded chemical companies, especially in China,
to make more HCFC-22.[384]

Even the alleviation of world hunger can be turned
into what appears to be a crony capitalist battleground.
A French company, Nutriset, in 2007 persuaded the
World Health Organization to endorse its Plumpy'nut
product for starving children, which costs $1 a day per
child and produces plentiful company dividends. The
company also patented its product, a peanut paste fortified with dried milk, vitamins, and other ingredients. Other firms have sued to invalidate the patent on
grounds that it is just fortified peanut butter.[385]

Legal and commercial battles, in which parties
try to win the support of governments and international organizations, are a familiar phenomenon.
What is less familiar is the ease with which foreign
special interests seem to be able to inject their money
into American political campaigns. In October 2010,
in the middle of Congressional elections, President
Obama accused the US Chamber of Commerce of

bringing foreign money into the campaign, a violation of the 1907 Tillman Act and further foreign donor restrictions passed in 1966 and 1976. The Chamber acknowledged some foreign funding, but denied that it was used for politics.[386]

It was remarkable for President Obama to make this charge, since at the same time larger amounts of foreign funds were pouring into US labor unions, which were working on Obama's side. Moreover, his administration had reversed a Bush administration rule making it harder for unions to hide the source and use of funds by setting up partially owned affiliates that are not subject to reporting. Thanks to the change made by Obama's Secretary of Labor, Hilda Solis, who had previously directed a labor union affiliated group, there was no way to know how much foreign union money was entering US politics through the union channel.[387]

It is also not widely known that a special group of foreign citizens, green card holders, have the legal right to donate to US political campaigns. Moreover, green cards can be "bought." If a foreigner agrees to invest $500,000 in the US, he or she receives a green card for two years. If after that period, the investment is deemed to have created ten jobs, the card will be extended and a path to citizenship opened. This EB-5 program has recorded $2.3 billion in "investments." The very existence of this program is of course an invitation for foreigners to become "friendly" with US politicians, and the best way to do that is to use the green card to make political donations.[388]

In his 2010 State of the Union address, President Obama said, "I don't think American elections should be bankrolled by America's most powerful interests, and worse, by foreign entities." There are many past examples of foreign governments attempting to fund US presidential campaigns.[389] But what about foreign small donors, a group that can now be tapped through the internet?

During the 2012 election campaign, it was discovered that the website Obama.com was owned by an American businessman living in China, with close ties to the Chinese government, who had been a frequent visitor at the White House, and who had been seated at the head table during a 2011 state dinner for the president of China. When online visitors arrived at his Obama.com site, they were immediately forwarded to an Obama campaign donation site, where they were asked for donations under $200 (donations above this level are supposed to be reported). In some instances, the individual was solicited repeatedly, but never for more than $200, and the usual e-commerce security guards that could be used to verify the donor and the donor's nationality were omitted. These security guards were used on the websites of Mitt Romney, Obama's opponent.[390]

In September of 2012, President Obama's campaign reported raising $181 million, with 98% of it from donations under $200 and therefore not reportable.[391] Inspired by this news, some reporters found they could contribute under the name Osama Bin Laden, with an obviously false foreign address and zip code. "Bin Laden" was even solicited by the campaign for additional small donations.[392]

How much of President Obama's 2012 campaign was financed by illegal foreign donations? It appears that some of it was, but we do not know how much, because neither the mainstream press nor prosecutors have chosen to pursue the story, even though the evidence is well documented.

Part Nine

Losers

25

Charity Gets No Respect

T HERE IS A common saying on Capitol Hill
that those who do not come to the table
will become the lunch. This refers to those
who fail to hire sufficiently well connected lobbyists
or make large campaign contributions. Even those
who do come to the table may get carved up. When
President Obama called the parties making money
from medicine into the White House to discuss what
would become of Obamacare, most of the special
interests tried to make a deal. With the Democrats
controlling Congress and the White House, they
knew that defiance would likely backfire.

The major insurance companies were not sure, and
bought a few attack ads, but they were immediately

threatened, and got in line. The only parties that did not "buy in" were the medical equipment manufacturers, and as a result the bill included a major tax increase on them, a tax increase big enough to wipe out the entire profit of some of them.

A group that does come to the table, but lacks much clout, is the nonprofit sector. There are some exceptions. Planned Parenthood is effective in Washington and receives federal funding, despite its controversial abortion services. Between 2003–2008, the organization received more than $2 billion in federal funds, of which the Government Accounting Office could only account for $657 million.[393] But in general the nonprofit sector is not seen as a lobbying powerhouse, if only because charities cannot legally make campaign contributions or participate in elections.

This may be why President Obama on several occasions after his election proposed to eliminate charitable gift tax deductions for high earners and why, toward the end of the 2012 presidential election and shortly thereafter, Mitt Romney and other Republicans appeared to join him. The Republicans were vague. But they spoke of preventing income tax rate increases by removing deductions, and the charitable deduction was one of the deductions on the chopping block.

Critics of this assault on charitable deductions for high earners noted that Presidents Bush and Obama had chosen to bail out auto companies and Wall Street. Why tear down the whole charitable sector? That sector represented about 11% of the economy. It employed 13.5 million people, about 10% of the workforce.

Did the president consider charitable work, most of it done at lower wages and benefits than found in government or business, less valuable? Or was it that charity workers, unlike auto workers, were not concentrated in presidential swing states? President Obama said about his "Jobs Bill" in 2011: "These aren't games we are playing here. Folks are out of work."[394] Well "folks" were out of work in the charitable sector too, yet ending the charitable deduction was part of how the president said he would pay for the Jobs Bill.

President Obama's proposal to curtail the ability of single people with incomes over $200,000 or families with incomes over $250,000 to take a tax deduction on charitable gifts was on top of another reduction (the "Pease limitation") that was already scheduled to come back with the end of the Bush tax cuts. He justified this in 2009 by saying, "I think [this] is a realistic way for us to raise some revenue from people who have benefited enormously over the last several years."[395] But that argument did not make any sense. Taking away the charitable deduction does not penalize the rich; it penalizes charities and the people being served by the charities. If the rich do not give, they end up with more money, not less. They do not suffer at all.

Obama's budget director at the time, Peter Orszag, seemed to acknowledge this—that it was the charities, not the big donors, who would suffer under this proposal[396]—when he said that charities should be willing to make this sacrifice in return for more people getting health insurance under the Patient Protection and Affordable Care Act ("Obamacare"). But this didn't make any sense either. First, yanking the charitable tax deduction was not part of the president's plan to finance broader healthcare. Second, reducing the deduction actually makes it harder to cover more people.

This last point only requires a moment's thought. As we have already noted in an earlier chapter, if you want to cover more people, you need more doctors and nurses and clinics. In economic terms, if you increase demand, you should increase supply. Otherwise, people with the new health coverage still won't be able to see a doctor or have to wait for weeks and weeks, and prices will likely soar.

This is not an abstract idea. It is has already happened in Massachusetts under Romneycare. Following implementation, newly covered people could not find a doctor, and prices were rising so rapidly that the legislature passed a price control system (even though price controls almost always fail). So if you need more healthcare supply nationally, how does it help to take a hatchet to nonprofit healthcare providers? In this context, it is

important to know that many of the healthcare providers in the US are nonprofit. This includes 62% of hospitals, 30% of nursing homes, and all of the healthcare
organizations (Mayo Clinic, Cleveland Clinic) that
President Obama has publicly praised as role models.

The president also said, "There is very little evidence that . . . [cutting the charitable deduction] has
a significant impact on charitable giving." In fact, the
evidence says the opposite, that for every 1% reduction in the deduction, gifts from wealthy people fall
1%.[397] That kind of drop in charitable giving would
be devastating for nonprofits. As David Harris, executive director of the American Jewish Committee,
wrote to the president, "Most nonprofits derive 70 to
80 percent of their donations from a small proportion of their donors who are major givers. This proposal will deal a major blow."[398]

Moreover, "taxing" major donors' gifts would not
even produce that much revenue for the government,
only an estimated $54 billion a year, not much com-
pared to $300 billion in tax subsidies for health insur-
ance or an overall budget deficit of $1.2 trillion. And
charities would be expected to lose at least $54 billion
and possibly much more. Will we really make America better by taking a dollar from charities and giving
it to government?

President Obama added that he does not think
it is fair that someone in the 35% tax bracket gets a

35% charitable deduction while someone in the 28% tax bracket gets a 28% deduction.[399] Of course, the employer tax deduction for health insurance works the same way (the higher your income, the bigger deduction you get), and it involves much more money. The president did nothing to change this in his healthcare legislation because unions did not want it changed.

Also, if fairness is so important, why was the Affordable Care Act set up so that families at the identical income level receive government insurance subsidies that vary by $10,000 or even as much as $20,000? That did not seem very fair.[400]

Furthermore, there is an easy fix to put everyone's tax treatment for charitable giving on the exact same footing. Independent Sector, representing nonprofits as a whole, has proposed that "charitable contributions should not be included in an individual's adjusted gross income (subject to tax)."[401] What would be even better: reduce tax dollar for dollar with gifts, which would treat everyone alike and produce a torrent of income for charities. If government chose not to go that far, it could at least provide a tax credit for charities that directly help the needy.

President Obama had seemed to be praising charities in his Democratic Convention acceptance speech.[402] He said, "We know that churches and charities can often make more of a difference than a poverty program alone." But looked at more closely, the words "often" and "more" are important qualifiers. The president was actually saying that charities do not always make a difference and if they do it is by adding to what government is already doing.

Judging from this remarkably backhanded compliment, it is possible that the president actually regards charities as competitors of government. Both, as he may see it, are in the business of helping people. If it is done through charity, there is no way to win votes in the process. If it is done through government, voter constituencies may be created, which is something that politicians may want, but which we as a society should reject.

Charity is not just another crony capitalist tool. To keep it free from this taint, we should reject another Peter Orszag proposal, that in exchange for eliminating the charitable deduction on large gifts, government would provide a 15% match on smaller charitable gifts.[403] Even Orszag admits that religious gifts would have to be excluded, and, realistically, that would only be the beginning. Once government started matching, it would be no time at all before government would start choosing eligible charities and directing ever more tightly how the money can be directed.

At the moment, without this kind of government interference, charitable programs for the poor are effective, much more effective than government programs, as the next chapter will discuss. Furthermore, charities offer a diversity of approaches. They are a laboratory of ideas and actions, something that the government can never be. They also represent people-to-people solutions, the democratic ideal in action.

Most countries do not have a thriving nonprofit sector. Europe does not have it, nor Japan. This has been a uniquely American phenomenon, recognized and encouraged by our tax laws. Now it is under attack and only time will tell if it survives.

26

The Poor

IN GENERAL, IF we are trying to help people in a sensible and moral way, there are at least three ways to go about it. One familiar way is develop government programs. Another is government funding of private charities. A third is building a thriving charitable sector, especially if charitable giving is supported by tax deductions, or even better, full credits.

One of the advantages of supporting charities is that they, unlike government, can make human and moral judgments. They can distinguish between what used to be called in the 19th century the "deserving" versus the "undeserving" needy. For example, in the category of those "undeserving" of help would be included anyone pretending to be disabled, something which government does not seem equipped to detect.

The federal disability program was founded under Social Security in 1956. In 1960, Congress removed a minimum age requirement, in 1965 allowed people to qualify with mental or musculoskeletal (e.g. back) problems, which are difficult to diagnose on an objective basis, and in 1984 liberalized the rules further. By 2010, mental and musculoskeletal cases represented 54% of all new applicants. To be accepted in the program, one can no longer work, and only 1% of those qualifying ever leave it.[404] After two years on disability, the enrollee also automatically qualifies for Medicare.

By 2012, 6% of the working-age population was enrolled, and received $270 billion in annual payments. The numbers increased after the Crash of 2008 but had grown rapidly for several decades at a rate far exceeding employment growth, so that fewer workers' taxes were available to support those not working. A Senate subcommittee investigation in 2012 found that applications were often passed without any real review, and appeals have also been very hard to lose.[405]

A Government Accountability Office study, also in 2012, found that 117,000 individuals were collecting both disability and unemployment insurance at a cost of $850 million. Indeed one individual cited was drawing disability, unemployment, and actually working. The reason that 117,000 could easily collect both disability and unemployment is that the checks are drawn by Social Security and the Labor Department, and no effort was made to cross check.[406]

The disability program has been variously described—by proponents as a vital social safety net, by critics as a backdoor replacement for welfare now that the welfare program has a five-year limit and work requirement, or even as a vote buying scheme. It is also strangely dissonant with the Americans with Disabilities Act of 1990. That Act states that the disabled are entitled to work and that employers may be sued for discriminating against them. Yet an employer with a disabled worker will save money if that worker moves into the federal disability program where work is not allowed. So, in effect, all the incentives are aligned to move workers into the program and none to move them out of it.

Although the growth in adult eligibility for the disability program has received press attention, very little has been said about the growth of child eligibility. Yes, children qualify also, and may be enrolled for ADHD (Attention Deficit Hyperactivity Disorder). Unfortunately this creates a strong incentive for impoverished parents to put their children on drugs like Ritalin and to discourage them from doing well in school.

As *New York Times* columnist Nicholas Kristoff, a political progressive, has written:

> This is what poverty sometimes looks like
> in America: parents here in Appalachian
> hill country pulling their children out of
> literacy classes. Moms and dads fear that
> if kids learn to read, they are less likely to
> qualify for a monthly check for having an
> intellectual disability.[407]

Of course it is often a mom or a dad, since the payment may be larger for a single parent. The typical payment for a disabled child is $698 a month, $8,376 a year, payable until age 18.[408]

The Food Stamp Program (SNAP) of the US Department of Agriculture is less controversial than Social Security disability, but still has its proponents and detractors, who variously describe it as a signal success or an out-of-control vote buying scheme. The program, which currently costs $47 billion a year, has been advertised by the Obama Administration on billboards and television. Government workers have even been sent into supermarkets to let shoppers know about it. As a result, one in seven adults now participate, one in four children, and one in five persons overall.[409]

Shortly after the 2012 presidential election, there were signs that the USDA was no longer promoting the program quite so energetically. In fact, only six days after the election, the *Toledo* (Ohio) *Blade*, located in the single most sought after "swing state," reported that food stamp benefits for state residents (and residents of some other states) would be significantly cut.[410] The timing of this announcement did not inspire confidence in the neutrality of the USDA.

Earlier the USDA had promoted the program as an economic stimulus program:

> SNAP is the only public benefit program which serves as an economic stimulus.... By generating business at local grocery stores, new SNAP benefits trigger labor and production demand, ultimately increasing household income and triggering additional spending.[411]

The economic theory behind this is fanciful,[412] but the USDA primarily works for agricultural-business interests, who benefit directly from Food Stamps, in addition to the intended beneficiaries, those who cannot afford food.

Besides giant agri-businesses and low income beneficiaries, various other constituencies either benefit or want to benefit from food stamps. These include both grocery stores and convenience stores, and USDA protects them by refusing to divulge food stamp sales by store or company or by what is bought. This especially suits the junk food industry since a great deal of junk food is bought in addition to candy and liquor. A shopper wrote his local newspaper in Vero Beach, Florida about what he saw being bought in a convenience store by a customer using a SNAP card: "a Red Bull energy drink [for the shopper and], a lollipop . . . , and KitKat bar [for an accompanying child]."[413]

Fast food restaurants (KFC, Taco Bell) complain about being left out and clamor to be allowed into the program.[414] There is also anecdotal evidence that food stamps are illegally traded for cash, but no government investigations have looked into the allegations. One Louisville woman was arrested for trying to buy an iPad with a food stamp card.[415]

Some people believe that both food and health-care should be "free" for all, by which they mean provided by government, and thus supported by taxing, borrowing, or printing money. The concept is even enshrined in the constitutions of several countries, including that of Mexico.[416] As we have discussed under healthcare, what this ignores is that if government guarantees food as a right, it will decide what food is provided, what food we may eat, who will profit from it, and by how much. In the end, special interests allied with government may carve out lucrative monopolies for themselves and have even greater control over consumer food choices.

In 2012, a video of an Ohio woman praising President Obama for providing free cell phones ("Obama-Phones" she called them) went "viral" on the web. Several websites, including Obamaphone.net, also promoted the phones. All this grew out of a 1984 government program called Lifeline, created to make landline phones available to low income Americans. In 2008, cell phones were added, the number of phones handed out began to rise, and so did cost, from $772 million in 2008 to $1.6 billion in 2011, by which time 17 million phones had been distributed. Costs are covered with a tax on everyone's phone bill, a tax that rises automatically with program expenditure. Few people notice the tax, so there are really no restraints on spending.

For much of the 2012 campaign, it was thought that whichever candidate carried Ohio would win the presidency. It therefore raised eyebrows when the *Dayton* (Ohio) *Daily News* reported that one million Ohioans had been given phones between first quarter 2011 and first quarter 2012, double the number from the prior year.[417] In addition, approximately half of the cell phones handed out nationally seem to have come from a single company, Tracfone, owned by Mexican billionaire Carlos Slim.

The CEO of Tracfone, F. J. Pollak, has been a large-scale donor to the Obama campaigns. His wife "bundled" more than $1.5 million in contributions and also personally contributed more than $200,000 to Democratic campaigns and committees 2008–2012.[418] After the election, Tracfone won a new contract from the Federal Communications Commission (FCC) to provide internet services to low income job seekers, although the company's cell phones seem better designed for video games and Facebook than for resume preparation or internet searches.[419]

The largest single "means tested" federal program is the Earned Income Tax Credit (EITC), which in 2011 applied to 27 million taxpayers and cost $60 billion, most of which took the form of cash payments made to workers, who earned below a minimum threshold ($40,000 a year for a family with two or more children). It has been estimated that approximately one fourth of the payments are "improper" for one reason or another. Even identity thieves have applied for it.[420] As of 2011, the smaller federal welfare program covering non-working individuals and families, Temporary Assistance for Needy Families, cost the federal government $36 billion in the form of block grants to the states, which bore the rest of the cost.

What is most curious about the Earned Income Tax credit is that, like Section 8 housing vouchers and Medicaid, it is excluded when calculating whether an individual or family falls below the official poverty threshold. Social Security disability and other cash payments are included, but these are not, even though EITC takes the form of a check or deposit. If they were included, the number of poor would be sharply reduced.

Looking at all federal and state welfare programs as a whole, the total spending per year comes to $61,194 per household below the official poverty line, as reported by a Senate subcommittee. This figure is misleading because it includes spending for those not in poverty, such as Pell grants for students, but is still almost three times the official 2011 national federal poverty threshold for a family of four, which is $22,350.[421] If medical programs are excluded, the total is still twice the 2011 poverty threshold.

Poverty statistics were redone right after the 2012 election. A new series based on location puts the threshold at $37,900 for a family of four in New York City.[422] But even with this radical revision, the numbers imply that a great deal of spending to help the poor is not reaching them, which implies that others, not poor, including government employees, are benefiting instead. If all this spending were simply given to the poor, it would probably pull everyone above the official poverty threshold. This is not necessarily a good idea, because it would pay people to be poor.

There is a further anomaly about most government poverty programs. They phase out as income increases. This imposes the equivalent of an enormous tax on the first dollars earned above the poverty threshold and a major disincentive to start up the economic ladder. As economist Thomas Sowell has explained:

> Someone who is trying to climb out of poverty by working their way up can easily reach a point where a $10,000 increase can cost them $15,000 in lost benefits they

no longer qualify for. That amounts to a marginal tax rate of 150 per cent—far more than millionaires pay.[423]

It is relevant to bring up millionaires in this context, because so many dollars of government welfare programs go to those who are not poor, including corporations and millionaires. An estimate of corporate welfare alone made in 2002 by the Cato Institute came to $92.6 billion, just a bit less than the EITC and TANF together.[424] In 2010, almost 2,400 millionaires (that is, people earning $1 million a year or more) received unemployment checks from the government, and had their unemployment checks extended, like everyone else's, from 26 weeks to 73 weeks by the end of 2012.[425] Shoppers at Sam's Club in 2010 were offered loans of up to $25,000 backed by the US Small Business Administration, loans that were clearly not meant for the poor.[426]

The big money, however, lies in mortgage guarantees, mortgage interest deductions, and Social Security and Medicare checks. As noted in an earlier chapter, federal agencies prior to the Crash of 2008 guaranteed "jumbo" mortgages of up to $729,750 for rich people, a figure later reduced to a mere $625,500, with the interest tax deductible for primary residences. Of the $1.5 trillion spent annually on entitlements, one estimate suggests that $200 billion could be saved by means testing them.[427]

Government checks of all kinds are estimated to reach half of all US households.[428] 18% of all personal income comes from this source.[429] And these government checks have grown significantly more under Republican than Democratic presidents.[430] By 2012, the value of future checks promised had grown to as much as $222 trillion, an increase of $11 trillion from a year earlier.[431] An increase in unfunded promises of $11 trillion in only one year may be compared to total federal spending of $3.7 trillion, total federal taxes of $2.5 trillion, and a 2011 annual gross domestic product of $15 trillion. By adding the total unfunded liabilities of $222 trillion to the acknowledged debt of the federal government, which is $13.4 trillion,[432] you get a total liability of $235 trillion, or 16 times GDP. And this excludes money the government owes itself and all state and local debt.

Given the dire fiscal situation of the US government, it can hardly make sense to continue borrowing money from China (or recklessly printing it) in order to pay corporate welfare or send entitlement checks to the affluent. But what about the truly needy? Most people want to help them. To return to the question that opened this chapter, what is the best way to do it?

Direct federal programs have a large downside. As noted, government does not seem capable of effectively administering its own programs. It also cannot and should not make moral distinctions about who deserves help and who does not, which charities can do. Moreover, any government program will bear the stigma of either real or imagined vote buying, of seeking to turn voters into junior cronies of politicians.

Acknowledging these handicaps, it would seem preferable to turn over the work of helping those in need to charities. This could be funded by direct government payments. Assuming that charities competed for federal funds on the basis of performance, this would both improve results and reduce the appearance of vote buying. However, this is not a good idea. There is too much risk of government and charities becoming cronies of each other, with crony services replacing results as the basis of selection.

The best solution, therefore, would be for government to fix one tax rate for all citizens that would fund the functions of government. A second tax bracket would apply to affluent taxpayers, but could be offset 100% by gifts to social service charities. This would produce a torrent of funds for charities competing to receive it. In effect, the nonprofit world would become a fully funded partner with the for-profit world and government.*

It would also be helpful to ask charities to tell us how many people in the US are poor, where they live, and

---

* For a more complete discussion of this concept, see Hunter Lewis, *Are the Rich Necessary? Great Economic Arguments and How They Reflect Our Personal Values* (Mr. Jackson, VA: Axios Press, 2009), concluding chapter.

what their needs are. Federal statistics on these subjects are both inadequate and misleading. For example, the government records income for households of unknown and changing size rather than individuals, omits federal payments such as earned income tax credits, takes no account of how many hours people work, and fails to tell us to what extent last year's poor are this year's poor.

In the long run, or even the not so long run, ending crony capitalism would do more than any other step to improve the condition of the poor. In the meantime we should fund the charitable sector to provide immediate relief.

27

War on the Young

SOME GROUPS ARE completely unrepresented at the table in Washington, and foremost among them are young people. The youngest do not vote at all, and those 18–29 years old have no group to represent them. This is in contrast to "seniors" who have a variety of groups representing them, including the powerful American Association for Retired People, although critics charge that AARP is more interested in its Medi-gap insurance business than in the interests of retired people.

Lacking any representation in Washington, young people have indeed been political losers. Consider this list of some of the many ways in which they lose from our current crony capitalist politics:

- They will inherit all the unpaid bills as federal deficits and unfunded liabilities soar. Economist Paul Krugman tells us that we are exaggerating this problem: "Talking about leaving a burden to our children is . . . nonsensical; what we are leaving behind is promises that some of our children will pay money to other children."[433] But half the debt is held by foreigners. In addition, as Michael Kinsley has pointed out: "The other children [Krugman refers to] will be the ones whose parents bought the bonds. In other words, the debt will turn into a giant redistribution program from the poor to the rich."[434]

- Poor young people already pay Social Security, Medicare, and other entitlement taxes in order to support all old people, including rich ones. Only 36% of federal transfer payments go to the bottom 20% of earners; most go to people better off than young taxpayers.[435] And households headed by 65-year olds or older have a net worth 47 times that of households headed by under 35-year olds.

- Obamacare made this situation even worse. In order to cover health insurance costs for older people, we are intentionally requiring young people to buy insurance they probably will not need. Moreover, legislation makes the cost of the insurance they are required to buy two to three times more expensive than it should be for their age.[436] This enormous cost shifting onto the backs of young

people far outweighs the much touted benefit of
allowing young people to stay on their parents policies until age 26.

- Obamacare also reduces available jobs, especially low
  wage jobs, which new labor force entrants such as
  young people might otherwise get. As we have previously noted, the required employer medical insurance contribution will add to the minimum wage at
  least $2.28 per hour (employee without family) or
  as much as $5.89 per hour (employee with family).
  Many employers will conclude they cannot afford
  this.[437] In addition, since most part-time workers do
  not count in calculating the penalty for an employer
  not providing health insurance, the number of full-
  time jobs available may also sharply contract.

  Unemployment in 2012 for young people under
  30 was already 17%, and would have been higher if
  many had not stopped looking for work.[438] Black
  teenage unemployment was 39%, which is also
  understated.[439] Would Obamacare have made this
  situation even worse if there had been a powerful
  American Association for Young People operating in
  Washington? Probably not. Yet voters under 30 voted
  67% for President Obama in the 2012 election.[440] If
  young people had simply divided their vote between
  the two candidates, Romney would have won, both
  nationally and in the key swing states such as Florida,
  Ohio, Virginia, and even Pennsylvania.

- After the election, in his State of the Union address, President Obama proposed an increase in the federal minimum wage to $9. Once again, young people were thrown overboard since, if enacted, the proposal would make the situation even more dire for those entering into the work force. Why was the proposal made? To please unions? Because it played well in focus groups or polls?

  The federal government apparently does not mind young people working as "interns" for nothing. These "intern" positions would almost certainly pay something if it were not for the minimum wage. And internships are only for the highly educated young. Less educated young are left to shift for themselves with no chance to get the first job that could give them the training and experience they need to start moving up the ladder.

- Just to make it a little worse, the US Department of Labor decided in 2012 that young college graduates would no longer be exempt from overtime in their jobs. How nice! New college graduates, no longer classed as professionals despite the effort and debt incurred to earn their degree, will be paid time and half for work over 40 hours—that is, if they got a job, since overtime pay further reduces their chances.[441]

- President Obama promised in 2008: "When I'm president, I will make college affordable for every American."[442] Instead, tuitions rose 25% and average student loan debt 16%.[443] The president campaigned in 2012 on the claim that he had held down the interest rate on student loans, a claim that, according to polls, resonated with young people. But, looking a little more closely, it does not hold up. The federal government borrows money at a negligible interest rate and re-lends it to students at the now reduced rate of 3.4%, thereby making a huge profit. The federal budget buries this profit in its financial statements under "deficit reduction." So students who will inherit all the loans generated by deficit spending are also supposed to kick in for the deficit now.

- President Obama also failed to mention that student loans were included in the spending that would automatically be cut in 2013 if a budget agreement were not reached with Republicans.[444] The president had personally framed the agreement this way, in part because he wanted to be sure that popular programs would be included if cuts automatically took place—the better to threaten Republicans with voter wrath. In effect, student loans, young people in general, were being used as hostages in political warfare.

- The student loan program also poses larger moral issues. Only about half of students in four-year colleges graduate after six years. Those who do not graduate have nothing to show for their debt.[445] The dropout rate can be even higher for two-year and trade programs, especially trade programs run by for-profits which live off government loan subsidies totaling more than $100 billion a year.[446]

When former students fail to repay their debts, they are often hounded by bill collection agencies hired by the US Department of Education. These agencies pursued an estimated 5 million borrowers owing $67 billion in the first nine months of 2011. They sometimes used abusive tactics and earned $1 billion for themselves.[447]

- In the 19th century, debt was portrayed in popular novels as a kind of slavery. If not slavery, is it not a form of indentured servitude? Is it right to saddle students just starting out in life with what has already grown to over $1 trillion in debt for all age brackets?[448] Of the current total, an estimated third is owed by those 40 or older.[449] Even individuals over 60 are currently struggling to pay $36 billion of student loans. Will today's young people ever be able to afford to start families or live a normal adult life?

- And what exactly do students get for all their debt? Traditional college programs do not necessarily prepare students for jobs or even help students find them. And all the federal subsidies are arguably making education less affordable, not more affordable. As Mark Zandi, chief economist at Moody's Analytics, has explained: "Universities and colleges just [use the subsidies to] raise their tuition [and other fees]."

Once again, it is the familiar story of supply and demand that we have already seen in medicine. When federal subsidies increase demand without changing supply, it just leads to higher prices. Online education may yet change the supply of educational options dramatically, so that educational costs fall. But that will not help today's students as they take on more and more debt, with ever less certainty of being able to repay it.

Part Ten

Democracy and Crony Capitalism

28

Is Democracy to Blame?

FOLLOWING THE CRASH of 2008, some influential voices began to suggest that democracy might lie at the root of our economic problem.

■ Here is Tom Friedman of the New York Times:

> One-party autocracy certainly has its drawbacks. But when it is led by a reasonably enlightened group of people, as in China today, it can also have great advantages. That one party can just impose the politically difficult but critically important policies needed to move a society forward in the 21st century. . . . [In America, on critical issues] only the Democrats are really playing. . . . There is only one thing worse than one-party autocracy, and that is one-party democracy, which is what we have in America today.[450]

This statement is all the more bizarre because China is itself a hotbed of crony capitalism. Its entire banking system is perennially insolvent; all the uneconomic loans flowing out to politically connected individuals, must be continually replenished by the government with newly printed money. When the Chinese Ponzi schemes collapse, as they eventually must, what will Friedman say then?

However, Friedman is not the only American establishment figure to wonder about democracy under current circumstances. Here are a few more:

- Governor, Bev Perdue (D-North Carolina), September 28, 2011:

  > I think we ought to suspend, perhaps, elections for two years and just tell [members of Congress] we won't hold it against them, whatever decisions they make, to let them help this country recover. . . . You want people who don't worry about the next election.[451]

- Evan Thomas, prominent journalist, writing in *Newsweek*, February 26, 2010:

  > The problem is . . . us—our "got mine" culture of [political] entitlement. Politicians, never known for their bravery, precisely represent the people.[452]

- Bob McKee, author of *Democrisis*, 2012:

    Democracy's a tired thing.[453]

- Paul Donovan, economist at UBS, 2012:

    I'm all in favor of . . . a benevolent dictatorship of economists.[454]

- Peter Orszag, President Obama's first budget director, 2011:

    Our democracy finds itself facing a deep challenge. . . . What to do? . . . We need to . . . rely . . . more on automatic policies and depoliticized commissions for certain policy decisions. In other words, radical as it sounds, we need to counter the gridlock of our political institutions by making them a bit less democratic.[455]

Orszag may have been thinking about The Independent Payment Advisory Board established under Obamacare to keep Medicare costs within pre-defined limits by restricting medical fees. As we have previously noted, each action of the Board automatically becomes law unless Congress—by a three-fifths super-majority in the Senate—votes a replacement measure that will reduce expenses by an equivalent amount. And Congress may only abolish the board by introducing legislation on or after January 2017, enacting it by August 15, 2017, with the abolition to be deferred until 2020.

In commenting on this new board, columnist George Will quotes British philosopher John Locke, whose ideas shaped the US Constitution:

> The legislative cannot transfer the power of making laws to any other hands. . . . The power of the legislature, being derived from the people . . . [is] only to make laws, and not to make legislators.[456]

In his message vetoing the recharter of the Second Bank of the United States, President Andrew Jackson argued that any such delegation of enumerated congressional powers violated the US Constitution itself. By permitting the establishment of what became in effect the Third Bank of the United States, renamed the Federal Reserve, the Supreme Court overruled Jackson—although a contemporary Supreme Court justice, Anthony Scalia, has vocally dissented from the many delegations that have followed. In the case of Obamacare and the Dodd-Frank Act that "strengthened" Wall Street regulation, even thousands of pages of statutory language have not sufficed, so that many of the most important provisions are written by executive agencies, not by Congress, and much of the implementation is either left to the discretion of the agencies or even turned over to boards similar to Obamacare's IPAB.

All of this follows a European pattern. Once the European Community was formed, more and more power migrated from democratically elected national governments to the center in Brussels, which is almost entirely run by the European Commission. This is a body of unelected officials whose decisions are rubber-stamped by a weak European Parliament comprised of members nobody takes seriously. The result has been a steady reduction in European democracy in favor of rule by "experts." The "experts" in turn are subjected, not to the discipline of elections, but to the daily blandishments of well-funded special interest groups, often represented by former Commission employees. One wonders how a principal author of these kind of undemocratic arrangements, British economist John Maynard Keynes, would have reacted to the new institutions. He had complained about "the mass of illiterate voters,"[457] and extolled the virtues of rule by "experts," but was not personally corrupt, and would not have been happy about the corruption that his own recommendations have helped bring into being.

No American presidential candidate has dared to criticize democracy directly, but some actions and words at least hint at reservations. When President George W. Bush announced his bail-out of Wall Street in the fall of 2008, polling revealed that it was deeply unpopular. GOP presidential candidate John McCain was at that moment essentially tied in the polls with Barack Obama, but was suffering from identification with his fellow Republican Bush. Had he opposed Bush's bail-out, the electorate might have gone with him. Instead, McCain, who knew little about economics, either thought he had a duty to oppose the voters or thought the voters would change their mind and thus sacrificed his chances.

Earlier in the same campaign, then candidate Obama had spoken to a small group of very wealthy donors at a San Francisco dinner and, in the course of his remarks, which he expected to remain private, described in unflattering terms the lower income workers in Pennsylvania and the Midwest who had rejected him:

> It's not surprising . . . that they get bitter, they cling to guns or religion or antipathy to people who aren't like them or anti-immigrant sentiment or anti-trade sentiment as a way to explain their frustrations.[458]

When later criticized for these patronizing remarks, which struck some observers as both elitist and antidemocratic, Obama was not exactly repentant:

> The underlying truth of what I said remains. . . . People feel like Washington's not listening to them, and as a consequence . . . rely on . . . faith . . . family, traditions like hunting. . . .[459]

This seemed to imply that people would not need religion, family, or a crude pastime such as hunting if they had the kind of government Obama would provide.

P. J. O'Rourke describes Barack Obama's elitism in these terms:

> Obama very much absorbed the lessons…
> [of] the 60s. While most of us who actually tried the 60s got over this, he didn't.…
> [He believes that] if you could just get the smartest people in the world together in a room, then by golly you can figure out a healthcare program. It's this kind of contempt for the ordinary person's expertise [about] what is best for him or her… that he took away from the 1960s in large bags and cartons.[460]

This describes only part of Obama's elitism. There is another side as well, a side that paradoxically conflicts with the Harvard notion of rule by the intelligentsia. Chicago politics is also in a sense elitist, because it's shady, crony capitalist deals are done behind closed doors, out of sight of press or voters, and then covered up as far as possible with clouds of dissembling (spin, half lies, plausible lies, even the occasional bald-faced big lie). But Chicago has a populist flavor too, because it is in-your-face and no respecter of persons. There is no way to reconcile the

Harvard social engineer and Chicago pol; Obama simply shifts from one to the other as convenient.

2012 GOP presidential candidate Mitt Romney did not sound so different. He spoke in the same condescending and elitist terms as President Obama when he met with a group of wealthy donors, also at what was supposed to be a private dinner, and referred to "47% of voters" who would not support him because they were "dependent upon government." He could have said that politicians were trying to buy their votes, which would not have got him into hot water, but instead appeared to blame the voters.

The implicit skepticism about voters' ability to make disinterested and sound judgments about where the country should go is certainly nothing new. It is the theme of Plato's *Republic*, a book with which America's founders were familiar. Would we be better off to entrust the country to 1,000 people chosen at random or to "more suitable" people? Jefferson and Jackson sided with "the people"; their political opponents either sided or were thought to side with the elite, which meant the wealthy. By the 20th century, the debate had subtly shifted, and as P. J. O'Rourke pointed out in his description of President Obama, the choice was now between "average people" and "smart people," or, in the usual formulation, "experts."

Herbert Croly, founder of the *New Republic* magazine, key organ of the American progressive movement, wrote that "the average American individual is morally and intellectually inadequate to a serious and consistent conception of his responsibilities as a democrat. . . ."[461] He also recommended that voters entrust the country to experts who would dispassionately "represent the national interest."[462]

This was complicated. Progressivism was supposed to be "for the people, not the powerful," as Democratic presidential candidate Al Gore intoned in his 2000 convention nomination acceptance speech. But "experts" would actually hold the power and call the shots. The reason these "experts," however powerful, were not to be confused with "the powerful," is that they represent a meritocracy, people chosen objectively from all races and regions and economic classes for their skills and knowledge, not an aristocracy based on birth, a plutocracy based on money, or an "old boys" network based on gender or ethnic background. Unpolluted by age-old iniquities of status-seeking and money grubbing, the meritocrats would bring "science" to bear on the nation's problems and find what Croly called "efficient" solutions.

In similar spirit, Edward House, President Wilson's chief advisor at the dawn of the new Progressive Age, wrote a novel titled *Philip Dru: Administrator*. As columnist George Will describes the book:

> With the nation in crisis, Dru seizes power, declares himself "Administrator of the

Republic," and replaces Congress with a commission of five experts who decree reforms that selfish interests had prevented.[463]

George Will does not think much of the idea of government by "expert" superseding, little by little, a constitutionally guided and restricted democracy. As a self-professed conservative, he agrees with philosopher George Santayana that "parties and governments are bad . . . in most ages and countries. . . ,"[464] and thinks they are all the worse when guided by self-appointed, social engineering elites epitomized by Tom Friedman, Peter Orszag, Barack Obama, or Mitt Romney. Other critics, not expressly conservative in their view, some libertarian, some simply populist, also challenge the wisdom of government by an "expert" elite. For example:

- Scott Rasmussen, respected political polling expert and author:

  > Both Romney and Obama highlighted the condescending attitude that political elites hold of the people they want to rule over. A *National Journal* survey found that 59 percent of political insiders don't think voters know enough to have meaningful opinions on the important issues of the day. That's a handy rationalization for those who want to ignore the voters and impose their own agenda.[465]

■ John Goodman, scholar and healthcare expert, speaking tongue-in-cheek:

> I'm glad we have an educated elite running the show.[466]

■ Noted scholar Charles Murray:

> The bubble that encases the New (American) Elite crosses ideological lines and includes far too many of the people who have influence, great or small, on the course of the nation. They are not defective in their patriotism or lacking a generous spirit toward their fellow citizens. They are merely isolated and ignorant. The members of the New Elite may love America, but, increasingly, they are not of it.
>
> [Their] politics... are not the main point. When it comes to the schools where they were educated, the degrees they hold, the zip codes where they reside, and the television shows they watch, I doubt if there is much to differentiate the staff of the conservative *Weekly Standard* from that of the liberal *New Republic*, or the scholars at the American Enterprise Institute from those of the Brookings Institution, or Republican senators from Democratic ones.[467]

- Scholar Angelo M. Codevilla:

  Ordinary people have gone a long way toward losing equal treatment under law. . . .
  Laws and regulations are nowadays longer
  than ever because length is needed to spec-
  ify how people will be treated unequally. For
  example, the healthcare bill of 2010 takes
  more than 2,700 pages to make sure that
  some [people] . . . will be treated differently
  from others . . . [and] to codify bargains. . . .

  The ruling class is united and adamant about
  nothing so much as its right to pronounce
  definitive "scientific" judgment on whatever
  it chooses. When the government declares,
  and its associated press echoes that "scientists" say this or that, ordinary people . . .
  lose any right to see the information that
  went into what [some] "scientists" say.[468]

  Although Charles Murray characterizes the 21st century American elite as "not lacking a generous spirit . . . ,
merely isolated and ignorant . . . ," others see a growing problem of selfishness and corruption:

- Economist Marc Farber:

  In the 1970s and 1980s, I visited numerous
  banana republics and what always struck
  me was the complete indifference the elite

displayed toward ordinary people. Sadly this seems now [2011] to be the case in the US as well.[469]

- Think Tank founder Jerry Bowyer:

  The [Bill] Daleys,... the [Robert] Rubins,... the Rahm Emanuels of the world who rotate out of commerce secretary, treasury secretary, White House chief of staff positions and into positions at the top of investment banks, government-regulated utility monopolies and various GSEs (government-sponsored enterprises) are our nomenklatura. They are the members of our permanent ruling class. They are tribute imposers. The fact that they wrap themselves in the rhetoric of street-level populism just means that they are poseurs in addition to being imposers. ...

  Increasingly our nation is divided, not between Rs [Republicans] and Ds [Democrats], but between TIs and TBs: tribute imposers and tribute bearers. The imposers are gigantic banks, agri-businesses, higher education Colossae, government employees, NGO (nongovernmental organization i.e. public affairs nonprofit) and QUANGO (quasi-autonomous nongovernmental organization, in this case, funded by, appointed

by, and advising government) employees
and the myriad others whose living is made
chiefly by extracting wealth from other
people. The bearers are the rest of us: the
people who extract wealth from the earth,
not from others.

What is the difference between crony capitalism and socialism? Not much.... Don't the favored people become rich under socialism?[470]

Such heterodox opinions are not popular in today's
establishment, the upper ranks of government, business, unions, the higher professions, and academe.
Although it prides itself on diversity, defined in racial
or ethnic terms, this establishment tends to be intol-
erant of diverse social or economic opinions. It still
believes in meritocracy and tries to live up to it, but
the ideal is easily lost among all the privileges.

Whatever their family origins, the children of the
well-educated are much more likely to become well-
educated themselves, even more likely than the children of the wealthy are to stay wealthy. Moreover,
privileged people, whether by birth or education or
wealth, can be just as foolish as others, if not more
so. If you doubt it, a good instructional manual is
historian Paul Johnson's book *Intellectuals*,[471] which
recounts the selfishness, self-indulgence, and folly of
some of the "great minds" of modern history.

Elitism is not a solution for real world problems. Democracy is not necessarily a solution either, but it does provide for the possibility of change. Yes, we should keep in mind economist Ludwig von Mises's sobering words:

> The masses are [not] always right [as some in the 19th century romantically believed].... "Belief in the common man" is no better founded than was belief in the supernatural gifts of kings.... Democracy ... cannot prevent majorities from falling victim to erroneous ideas and from adopting inappropriate policies which not only fail to realize the ends aimed at but result in disaster.[472]

This is true. It is also true that elite crony capitalists will try to "buy" the electorate by offering them small crumbs from the crony banquet table. They may seem to succeed for a time. But like all parasites, they depend on the continuing health of their host, in this case the economy. And as crony capitalist policies and practices sicken the economy, the money with which to try to buy the electorate becomes scarcer. At the moment, the federal government of the US enjoys unlimited money, because the US Federal Reserve is printing enough new money to cover the entire budget deficit. But that is not sustainable either. Neither buying votes nor debasing the currency can go on forever. Eventually the crony techniques will self-destruct, albeit after having done untold damage.

In the meantime, giving more power to elites who benefit, often directly, from crony capitalism, is not likely to solve crony capitalism. It is through democracy, and only through democracy, that corrupt elites can be overthrown without resorting to violence. Already many people, many voters are slowly waking up to the fictions they have been fed, and calling for radical change.

Some of the advocates for change are disgusted and now renegade members of the elite. Many more are just ordinary people. They understand that you cannot get something for nothing, that you cannot keep borrowing and spending and printing money forever, and that all the borrowing and printing and spending is mostly supporting a privileged few, not themselves.

These emerging populists, critics rather than proponents of "progressivism," now that "progressivism" has ossified into yet another form of elitism, may not yet know exactly what changes they want, or even how to separate fact from all the fiction. They may not yet know whom to trust. But they represent a wave of discontent, and that wave of discontent could yet evolve into a powerful force for reform.

However bad things have become, the new populist forces may yet prevail and roll back today's crony capitalist system. If so, it will be the people who have done it, not elitists urging less democracy, and more delegation of power to "experts." That is not the "change" we need. That is just repeating past mistakes and protecting the current corrupt regime.

Part Eleven

Solutions

29

Diagnosis

To BEGIN WITH, it may be helpful to summarize the most salient features of today's crony capitalist economic system:

1. Crony capitalism is not just a manifestation of private greed. It often arises as an unintended consequence of good intentions and idealistic impulses.

   As this author has written in *Free Prices Now!*, the companion volume to this one:

   > Fearful of private greed, wanting what is best for all, we bring government into ever more minute management of economic as well as political affairs. But in doing so, we do not strengthen our community. Instead we create an epidemic of lying, cheating, theft, and corruption, with more and

more people trying to get something for nothing, relying not on what they can do, but on whom they know in government. In surprisingly little time, all the bonds of trust and cooperation nurtured by the free price system become frayed or just disintegrate.[473]

2. The growing government required to run the economy eventually becomes too big to be financed by taxes. It then relies on central banks, including the US Federal Reserve, to finance itself.

The US Federal Reserve finances government expansion in a variety of ways:

- By blowing up economic bubbles with newly printed money, it increases tax revenues, at least until the bubbles burst.

- By repressing interest rates, it enables government to borrow at rates that may be even less than consumer price inflation, which in turn makes it feasible to borrow almost unlimited amounts of money.

- By printing new money that is then used, directly or indirectly, to buy government bonds.

Thibault de Saint Phalle, author of *The Federal Reserve: An Intentional Mystery* (1985) showed how the Fed was financing government deficits even before the huge (and arguably illegal) expansion of its powers by Chairman Ben Bernanke after the Crash of 2008:

> The Fed, by financing the federal deficit year after year, makes it possible for Congress to continue to spend far more than it collects in tax revenue. If it were not for Fed action, Congress would have to curb its spending habits dramatically.[474]

3. A growing government, taking more and more control of the economy without actually owning it, as in socialism, makes deals with powerful special interests, as per the following list, which we have already seen:

What Private Interests Want from Government

- Exemption from legislation—e.g., NRA/Sierra Club in Campaign Finance Bill
- Favorable legislation—e.g., UPS/FedEx battle in Congress, Card Check, proposal to let unemployed sue, rum interests
- Sales—e.g., defense, drugs, vaccines, school lunches
- Regulatory changes—e.g., health, drugs, housing, banking, financing, agriculture, food, autos,

broadcasting, railroads, insurance, trucking, airlines, education, energy, law, accounting

- Exemption from regulation—e.g., Obamacare, waivers, family offices under Dodd-Frank, flame retardants

- Regulation that discourages new or small competitors—e.g., drugs, supplements, generic drugs, slaughter houses, healthcare

- Influence over price controls—e.g., State of Massachusetts medical

- Access to credit—e.g., green energy, housing, Wall Street

- Access to cheap credit—e.g., banking, housing, finance

- Extension of monopoly status—e.g., patents and copyrights

- Monopoly status—e.g.,, drugs, unions, National Football League, securities rating services

- Noncompetitive bidding or contracts—e.g., vaccines

- Direct subsidies—e.g., education, including unionized teacher salaries, unions, auto, agriculture, junk food, ethanol, green energy, vaccines, housing (mortgages), AMA, earmarks, high speed rail, fast internet service

- Indirect subsidies—e.g., law and accounting both expand with regulations, AARP, Wall Street consultant after Crash, GMO food sales to farmers and abroad, mammograms, health insurance mandate

- Bail-outs—e.g., banking, finance, autos, Goldman Sachs

- Influence on reversal or phase-out of rescue or subsidy—e.g., electronic records companies, collection of union dues

- Promise of future bail-out (which reduces current cost of credit)—e.g., banking, housing, finance

- Protection from competitors, domestic or foreign

- Protection from prosecution—e.g., Goldman Sachs, drug companies, vaccine makers, GM bondholders

- Licensing—e.g., broadcasting, medical, most professional services, airlines, drugs, law, accounting

- Tariffs—e.g., sugar, sugar ethanol

- Avoid punitive measures—e.g., medical device makers in Obamacare

- Favorable price contrast restrictions—e.g., Fed control of interest rates, price of farm crop insurance, price of milk, Medicare prices, Medicaid, Obamacare Payment Advisory Board

- Targeted tax breaks—e.g., In 2009 stimulus bill for Hollywood and World War II Filipino veterans
- Modifications of tax penalties, deductions, clawbacks, or phase-outs—e.g., Pease deductions, Bush tax cuts, loss of subsidies when income rises, in effect a tax on work
- Prestigious public appointments

What Public Officials Want from Private Interests

- Campaign contributions
- Direct campaign assistance
- Indirect campaign assistance
- Assistance with "messaging"
- Money (illegal if a bribe, but not necessarily in other cases, e.g. assistance with a loan or access to a "sweetheart" investment)
- Support from "foundations" related to campaign contributors
- Regulatory fees to support agency jobs
- Jobs for friends, constituents, or eventually themselves
- Travel, entertainment, other "freebies"
- Power, control, and deference

The alliances and relationships formed between public officials and private interests may be counter-intuitive. A company may give more campaign money to a potentially hostile legislator than to a friendly one, in order to forestall trouble.

4. All these crony capitalist deals not only introduce lying, cheating, and corruption into the economic system. From a purely economic point of view, they also interfere with free economic prices and profits, the signals on which any economy relies. The result is economic chaos as well as corruption. Hobbled prices, linked to growing corruption, are enough to destroy any economy. Nor is it possible to restrain corruption without allowing truthful, unfettered prices. Oystein Dahle, a Norwegian businessman, perceptively noted that "the Soviet Union collapsed because it would not allow prices to tell the economic truth."[475]

With this brief summary in mind, we will now turn in the final chapter to a proposal for thorough, root and branch reform of our economic system.

30

Prescription*

FROM TIME TO time, many proposals are made to control crony capitalism. Some of them have great merit, including these:

- Forbid former government employees to lobby the agencies where they previously worked;

- Forbid government wages to be siphoned into political campaigns via public employee union dues;

- Give all union members control over the use of their dues for political purposes;

---

* Parts of this chapter also appear, with modification, at the conclusion of *Free Prices Now!*, this book's companion volume. *Free Prices Now!* provides a more complete account of why we need to free prices from government control within the economy in order to overcome the plague of crony capitalism.

- Forbid political contributions by government contractors, grant recipients, and employees;
- Require disclosure of all political campaign donations along with the source of independent campaign expenditures;
- Require disclosure of all loans and terms or other financial assistance to public officials;
- Require recusal, with no waivers, by all public employees on matters pertaining to a former employer, whether the work was done as an owner, employee, or contractor;
- Re-instate the Glass-Steagall prohibition against federally insured banks engaging in investment banking or speculation for their own account;
- Restore and increase bank reserve requirements;
- Prohibit "too big to fail" rescues of financial or other companies;
- Separate food and drugs within the FDA and either attach dietary supplements to food or give them their own agency with its own rules;
- Forbid the FDA and FTC from censoring the dissemination of solid, peer-reviewed science by vendors of products;
- Restore consumer choice in medicine;
- Prohibit government-industry partnerships in vaccines;

- Repeal and then radically simplify the present tax system, which is currently used to reward political allies and punish opponents;

- Forbid regulatory agencies from assuming an executive, legislative, and judicial role, thereby making a mockery of constitutional separation of powers;

- Require specific Congressional approval of all government regulations;

- Sunset new laws and regulations to ensure review;

- Limit medical malpractice and other corrupted tort awards;

- Abolish government-sponsored "private" enterprises such as Fannie Mae and Freddie Mac and end government control of the mortgage market;

- Turn over the development and implementation of public assistance programs to charities to ensure that they cannot be used as vote buying schemes, to allow greater flexibility and creativity, and in general build the charitable sector to become a co-equal with business and government. Provide a charitable tax credit to accomplish this.

These ideas are important. Some of them are big ideas. Enacting any of them would make a real difference. In addition, there are other useful steps that could be taken. At the same time, no such list of incremental changes will be enough. What our society and

336 CRONY CAPITALISM IN AMERICA

economy need at this point is a truly systemic reform that will strike crony capitalism at the roots.

This systemic reform will take government out of the business of influencing, manipulating, or controlling market prices. The crony capitalist system depends on these price manipulations; they are what private interests buy and what public officials sell. Crony capitalism will wither without them. As it withers, corruption will subside. The economy will recover and thrive. Jobs will once again be available for those able to work. Free prices must therefore be the banner under which today's reformers march.

Free prices should not be confused with an abandonment of legitimate principles of social justice. Our original constitutional system embraced the ideal of government as social and economic umpire, enforcing the rules against force and fraud and disavowal of contracts. Banning child labor or inhuman working conditions is legitimately part of the umpire's role and does not interfere with prices. The early laissez-faire reformers generally agreed. British Member of Parliament Richard Cobden (1804–1865), one of the principal leaders of the movement, wanted to get government out of a leadership role in the economy. But he voted for restrictions on child labor as well as for more child education. Like other laissez-faire reformers, he also fought for broadening the right to vote, the removal of restrictions on Jews, and against slavery.[476]

Our constitutional system was never perfect. As previously noted, the first law passed by Congress was an import Tariff Act which both interfered with prices and rewarded special interests, the crony capitalists of the day. But over time, the early mistakes were compounded by the wholly fallacious belief that government could improve on the free price system by controlling and manipulating it, indeed by subverting it. What a paradoxical doctrine, that the economy can be improved by destroying the price mechanism on which it depends.

Ben Bernanke, chairman of the Fed, would superficially seem to agree. He tells students in a university economics class that "prices are the thermostat of an economy. They are the mechanisms by which an economy functions."[477] But then he radically expands the price fixing reach of the Fed from short-term interest rates to all kinds of interest rates.

At the same time, the federal government, supported and financed by the Fed, expands its own price manipulations, monopolies, and subsidies, even adding a "fall-back" price control feature to the Affordable Care (Obamacare) Act. Some state governments follow suit: Massachusetts amends its "Romneycare universal health plan" by passing a medical price control law in 2012, a law that requires government approval not only of price changes, but of all "material" changes by healthcare providers.[478] In each case, price controls are expanded as a remedy for ills created in the first place by earlier price controls.

These are obvious examples, but on close examination almost everything the government does in trying to lead the economy involves a price manipulation or control. It is time to pay heed to some sensible advice from humorist P. J. O'Rourke: "[The free price system] is a bathroom scale. We may not like what we see when we step on the bathroom scale, but we can't pass a law making ourselves weigh 165. . . ."[479]

A thriving economy is comprised of billions of prices and trillions of price relationships. Left alone, these prices almost miraculously coordinate demand with supply so that buyers can obtain as much as possible of what they want. Refusing to let prices fall or pushing them higher (2% a year, now 2.5% a year, per the Fed's announced target, linked to an artificial and dubious index) is like jamming a stick into the spokes of a wheel or pouring sand into the fuel tank of an engine. If we do this, we should not wonder if the wheel ceases to turn or the engine refuses to run.

A successful society is a cooperative society. A cooperative society is an honest society. By far the most reliable barometer of economic honesty is to be found in prices. Honest prices, neither manipulated nor controlled, provide both investors and consumers with reliable economic signals. A corrupt, crony capitalist economic system does not want honest prices, honest information, or honest results. The truth may be inconvenient or unprofitable for powerful government leaders or private interests allied with them.

We need to allow prices to tell the truth, free from the self-dealing and self-interested theories that stand in their way. Any proposed government action in the economy should be evaluated on this one criterion at least: does it confuse, manipulate, or control prices? If it does, it should be rejected.

Is it possible that this one reform proposal—free prices applied logically, systematically, and courageously—can free us from the crony capitalist corruption and economic stagnation of the past, thereby opening up an economic future for everyone, not just the rich and powerful? Yes it is. Even the arch enemy of free prices, economist John Maynard Keynes, agreed that "ideas rule the world."[480]

It was not so long ago that humanity condemned economic competition and described economic change as evil. No wonder economic progress was unknown. Born poor, we died poor, with the limited exception of those few who controlled weapons and could take what they wanted, although under this system there was not much to take. It was the gradual discovery of the power of free prices, beginning especially before the so-called industrial revolution, that allowed for the advancement of living standards even with population growth.

That revolution remains tragically unfinished today. Indeed, it is in danger of being extinguished altogether by a resurgence of crony capitalism and controlled prices. But for our own sake, for the sake of the poor, and for the sake of our descendants, it is time to rediscover truth and re-commit to reform.

Endnotes

1. *Economist* (March 21, 2009): 57–58.

2. *Economist* (December 5, 2009): 73.

3. David Ignatius, Palatial Corruption, Russian Style, *Washington Post*, http://www.realclearpolitics.com (December 23, 2010).

4. http://www.reuters.com (August 28, 2012).

5. P. Johnson, *Forbes* (October 22, 2012): 36.

6. *Economist* (December 19, 2009): 149.

7. *Washington Times* (November 2, 2009): 37.

8. Ibid., 24.

9. Alan Beattie, *False Economy: A Surprising Economic History of the World*, http://www.bloomberg.com Review (April 16, 2009).

10. *Economist* (February 27, 2012): 27–29.

11. Michael Grunwald, *Washington Post* (December 27, 2002): A–10.

12. Bernholz (2003): 8.

13. *New York Review* (April 9, 2009): 20.

14. http://www.realclearpolitics.com (September 2, 2010).

15. George Reisman, post on http://www.mises.org (November 22, 2011).

16. Acemoglu et al, MIT, *The Value of Political Connections in the United States*, May 2009, revised December 2010.

17. http://www.bloomberg.com (October 27, 2009).

18. White House Meets Lobbyists Off Campus, http://www.politico.com (February 24, 2011), also *Washington Times* (July 5, 2010): 35.

19. Quoted in Robert Higgs, *Crisis and Leviathan*, (Oxford, 1987), 243.

20. P. J. O'Rourke, *Weekly Standard* (June 1, 2009): 10.

21. *Washington Times* (August 23, 2010): 29.

22. Johns Hopkins economist Steve Hanke, speaking on BBC (December 21, 2012).

23. *Washington Times* (August 20, 2011): 36.

24. *Washington Times* (June 15, 2009): 38.

25. http://www.wsj.com (May 5, 2011).

26. *Politico* (October 3, 2011).

27. Taibbi, *Rolling Stone* (March 3, 2011): 51.

28. http://www.yahoo.com (September 27, 2011) and http://www.hoover.org (September 27, 2011).

29. *Politico* (June 28, 2012).

30. *Vanity Fair* (April 2010): 142 and http://www.opensecrets.org, accessed August 13, 2012.

31. http://www.againstcronycapitalism.org (November 14, 2011).

32. http://www.nytimes.com (January 7, 2011).

33. http://pbs.org/newshour (January 22, 2010).

34. *Washington Times* (October 12, 2009): 3.

35. *Washington Times* (December 28, 2009): 7.
36. *Washington Times* (December 19, 2010): 35 and *New York Times* (July 5, 2010): A-1.
37. http://www.washingtonpost.com (January 12, 2012).
38. http://www.bloomberg.com (September 14, 2010), updated 2012.
39. http://www.thehill.com (October 1, 2012).
40. *Washington Times* (June 20, 2011): 7.
41. *Washington Times* (November 2, 2009): 3-13.
42. Dick Morris and Eileen McGann, http://www.townhall.com (March 11, 2009).
43. Strieff, http://www.redstate.com (September 20, 2012).
44. *Washington Times* (December 21, 2009).
45. *Grant's Interest Rate Observer* (May 30, 2008): 3.
46. *Forbes* (March 15, 2010): 27.
47. David Reilly, *Bloomberg News* (April 25, 2009).
48. *Atlantic* (March 2009): 55, re: the work of economist Andrew Oswald.
49. *Washington Times* (October 6, 2008): 34.
50. Senate Banking Committee (July 11, 2008).
51. http://www.cnsnews.com (June 6, 2011).
52. *New York Times* (August 19, 2012).
53. http://www.bloomberg.com (August 15, 2010).
54. *Grant's Interest Rate Observer* (November 16, 2012): 2.
55. *Grant's Interest Rate Observer* (April 6, 2007): 10.
56. *Grant's Interest Rate Observer* (November 28, 2008): 2.
57. *Forbes* (August 11, 2008): 19.
58. http://www.archierichards.com (October 1, 2008).
59. *Washington Times* (September 29, 2008): 34.
60. David R. Sands, *Washington Times* (September 29, 2008): 34; (February 9, 2009).

61. *Washington Times* (August 20, 2012).
62. *Washington Times* (August 20, 2012): 30 and (October 4, 2010): 34.
63. *Washington Times* (October 4, 2010): 34.
64. *Washington Times* (April 11, 2011): 33; (January 10, 2011): 31; and (February 8, 2010): 29.
65. *Washington Times* (October 25, 2010): 20.
66. http://www.againstcronycapitalism.org (December 2, 2011).
67. Ibid., (October 17, 2011).
68. *Washington Times* (March 21, 2011): 33.
69. David Boaz, http://www.realclearpolitics.com (January 29, 2009).
70. George Mason University study quoted in *Washington Times* (January 11, 2010): 33.
71. Ibid.
72. Ibid.
73. Ibid.
74. *Washington Times* (September 20, 2012): 21.
75. *Washington Times* (September 3, 2012): 23.
76. http://www.abcnews.go.com (January 1, 2012).
77. Bastasch, http://www.dailycaller.com (November 2, 2012).
78. *Washington Times* (May 30, 2011): 10 and 36.
79. *Washington Times* (December 5, 2011): 7.
80. http://www.publicintegrity.org (November 28, 2010).
81. Marc Thiessen, http://www.aei-ideas.org (September 15, 2012).
82. Ibid.
83. http://www.factcheck.org, a project of the Annenberg Public Policy Center (October 7, 2011).

84. *Washington Post* (January 4, 2012).

85. http://www.againstcronycapitalism.org (December 5, 2011).

86. *Washington Times* (October 15, 2012): 10.

87. Ibid.

88. truth-o-meter, http://www.politifact.com (September 25, 2012).

89. Ibid and http://www.washingtonpost.com (January 8, 2011).

90. http://www.againstcronycapitalism.org (January 19, 2012).

91. Nancy Pfotenhaver, http://www.usnews.com (July 23, 2012).

92. Ibid.

93. Gehrke, http://www.washingtonexaminer.com (January 17, 2013).

94. Ibid.

95. http://www.stossel.blogs.foxbusiness.com (February 24, 2011).

96. http://www.wsj.com (October 30, 2012).

97. http://www.againstcronycapitalism.org (November 2, 2011).

98. Solomon, http://www.washingtonguardian.com (October 31, 2012).

99. Poor, http://www.dailycaller.com (November 7, 2012).

100. *Washington Times* (October 26, 2012).

101. *Forbes* (August 6, 2012): 102-105.

102. Gehrke, http://www.washingtonexaminer.com (December 20, 2012); Horowitz, http://www.redstate.com (December 17, 2012); Staff, http://www.freebeacon.com (December 13, 2012).

103. Stossel, http://www.newsmax.com (November 9, 2012).

104. Ferrara, http://www.forbes.com (December 22, 2012); quoting Investors Business Daily (November 9, 2012).

105. Baum, http://www.bloomberg.com (December 5, 2012).

106. Carney, http://www.washingtonexaminer.com (January 2, 2013 and January 3, 2013).

107. Byrne. http://www.chicagotribune.com (January 8, 2013).

108. Crony Capitalist Blowout, http://www.onlinewsj.com (January 2, 2013).

109. *Harvard Magazine* (November 12, 2011): 40.

110. Mathew Mitchell, George Mason University, http://www.mercatus.org (July 8, 2012).

111. David Henderson, http://www.econlog.econlib.org (July 27, 2012), also Robert Caro's *The Years of Lyndon Johnson.*

112. http://www.freebeacon.com, quoted in http://www.againstcronycapitalism.org (August 21, 2012).

113. http://www.washingtontimes.com (October 10, 2011).

114. *Washington Times* (August 17, 2009): 38.

115. World Net Daily, http://www.wnd.com (January 29, 2010).

116. *Washington Times* (February 8, 2010).

117. *Washington Times* (December 21, 2009): 7.

118. http://www.weeklystandard.com, The Blog (March 22, 2013).

119. John Stossel, http://www.townhall.com (March 27, 2013).

120. *Newsweek* (June 22, 2009): 45.

121. http://www.1600fund.com (December 24, 2012).

122. Ibid.

123. *Washington Times* (July 5, 2010): 35.

124. *Washington Times* (December 17, 2012): 11.

125. http://www.usatoday.com (March 8, 2012).

126. *Washington Times* (August 8, 2011): 3.

127. *Washington Times* (November 1, 2010): 11.

128. http://www.anh-usa.org (July 31, 2012).

129. *Washington Times* (December 14, 2009): 3.

130. Manu Raju, Revolving Door for Healthcare Aides, http://www.politico.com (September 15, 2009).

131. Zajac, http://www.bloomberg.com (January 15, 2013).

132. http://www.foxnews.com (May 15, 2012).

133. http://www.factcheck.org, a project of the Annenberg Public Policy Center.

134. Carney, http://www.washingtonexaminer.com (January 22, 2013).

135. *Washington Times* (August 31, 2009): 33.

136. http://www.washingtonpost.com (May 8, 2012).

137. http://www.againstcronycapitalism.org (October 11, 2011).

138. http://www.cbsnews.com (September 3, 2012); *Bloomberg News* (March 8, 2011); http://www.washingtonexaminer.com (June 6, 2011); http://www.independent.co.uk (August 19, 2012).

139. T. Carney, *The Examiner* (April 21, 2010).

140. http://www.bloomberg.com (October 14, 2009).

141. http://www.nypost.com (April 21, 2010).

142. http://www.losangelestimes.com (April 6, 2010).

143. *Politico* (April 21, 2010).

144. http://www.opensecrets.org.

145. *Vanity Fair* (January 2010): 127.

146. http://www.bloomberg.com (December 21, 2009).

147. *Vanity Fair* (November 2009): 177.

148. *Rolling Stone* (May 26, 2011): 44.

149. http://www.mcclatchydc.com (November 1, 2009).

150. *Rolling Stone* (March 3, 2011): 50.

151. T. Carney, *The Examiner* (April 21, 2010).

152. *Rolling Stone* (May 26, 2011): 46.

153. http://www.thedailybeast.com (May 6, 2012).

154. Ibid. (August 14, 2012).

155. *Washington Times* (April 30, 2012): 36.

156. http://www.thedailybeast.com (May 6, 2012).

157. http://www.bloomberg.com (August 31, 2012).

158. http://www/bloomberg.com (December 1, 2009).

159. *Vanity Fair* (December 2012): 128.

160. http://www.economix.blogs.nytimes.com (April 14, 2011).

161. http:///www.washingtonexaminer.com (June 5, 2011).

162. *Vanity Fair* (January 2010): 128.

163. Charlie Rose CBS interview, http://www.freebeacon.com (December 10, 2012).

164. *Grant's Interest Rate Observer*, (October 5, 2012): 1.

165. Carney, http://www.washingtonexaminer.com (January 2, 2013).

166. http://www.washingtonexaminer.com (February 2, 2011).

167. http://www.againstcronycapitalism.org (February 21, 2012).

168. *Times of London*: also http://www.washingtonexaminer.com (May 17, 2011).

169. http://www.anh-usa.org (October 12, 2010).

170. Ibid., (August 21, 2012); and Genetically Engineered Foods FAQ.

171. Ibid., (September 11, 2012).

172. Ibid.; Genetically Engineered Foods FAQ.

173. Michael Hawthorne, *Chicago Tribune* (September 10, 2012).

174. Oral History interview, Ruckelshaus article, http://www.wikipedia.org.

175. http://www.huffingtonpost.com, (January 28, 2010).

176. Viola Goode Liddell, *With a Southern Accent* (Norman, OK: University of Oklahoma Press, 1948): 111–112.

177. George Mason University, http://www.mercatus.org (August 19, 2012).

178. http://www.anh-usa.org, (December 21, 2010).

179. *Washington Times* (December 16, 2012): 18.

180. http://www.against.cronycapitalism.org (December 21, 2011).

181. Walter E. Williams, http://www.townhall.com (August 17, 2010).

182. www.mercola.com (February 4, 2012); American Enterprise Institute website, accessed September 10, 2012.

183. Ibid., American Enterprise Institute, see http://www.americanboondoggle.com.

184. Senate investigative panel, *Washington Times* (November 8, 2010): 10.

185. http://www.mercola.com (February 4, 2012).

186. Apples to Twinkies, http://www.uspirg.alphapirg.org (September 2011).

187. http://www.washingtonexaminer.com (August 15, 2012).

188. John Goodman, http://heathblog.ncpa.org (December 17, 2012).

189. Goodman, http://healthblog.ncpa.org (September 19, 2012); (March 31, 2012).

190. Gary Null, *Death by Medicine* (Mt. Jackson, VA: Praktikos Books, 2011).

191. Goodman, http://healthblog.ncpa.org (January 7, 2013).

192. Ibid.

193. Goodman, http://healthblog.ncpa.org (September 5, 2012).

194. Ibid., (January 22, 2012).

195. Pettypeice, http://www.businessweek.com (November 21, 2012).

196. http://www.emedicaresupplements.com (2012).

197. Goodman, http://healthblog.ncpa.org (August 27, 2012).

198. Ibid., citing Aaron Carroll (August 15, 2012).

199. Peter Orszag, *Foreign Affairs* (July/August 2011), 45–46.

200. George Will, *Washington Post* (May 12, 2011).

201. Goodman, http://healthblog.ncpa.org (July 16, 2012).

202. Ibid., (July 30, 2012).

203. Ibid., (April 18, 2012).

204. Ibid., (June 25, 2012).

205. Ibid, (September 5, 2012).

206. Ibid., (August 8, 2012).

207. Ibid., (January 11, 2012).

208. Ibid., (October 1, 2012).

209. George Will, *Washington Post* (October 4, 2012).

210. Ibid., (November 9, 2012).

211. Craig Smith, http://www.anh-usa.org (February 26, 2013).

212. Medicare Bills Rise as Records Turn Electronic, *New York Times* (September 21, 2012).

213. Smith, http://www.anh-usa.org (February 26, 2013).

214. Malkin, *Washington Times* (December 24, 2012): 33.

215. Malkin, http://www.townhall.com (December 14, 2012).

216. http://www.weeklystandard.com (October 8, 2012).

217. Bad Pharma, *The Economist* (September 29, 2012).

218. Voreacos, http://www.bloomberg.com (November 12, 2012).

219. Bad Pharma, *The Economist* (September 29, 2012).

220. *Forbes* (September 24, 2012): 80.

221. http://www.againstcronycapitalism.org (February 9, 2012).

222. *Natural News* (May 28, 2012).

223. *Wall Street Journal* (June 17, 2012): A–19.

224. *New York Times* (July 28, 2009): A–18.

225. http://www.veritasvirtualvengeance.com (January 9, 2012).

226. *Washington Times* (February 21, 2011): 37.

227. http://www.vaccinesafetycouncilminnesota.org (September 24, 2011).

228. http://www.anh-usa.org (September-October 2011 e.g. September 20, 2011).

229. David Kirby, http://www.huffingtonpost.com (March 29, 2008).

230. http://www.mercola.com (September 4, 2012).

231. Ibid., (July 10, 2012).

232. http://www.gao.gov/products/GAO-11–435.

233. Ibid., (June 2011); Rob Stein, *Washington Post* (November 24, 2009).

234. John Carey, *Bloomberg* (April 28, 2009).

235. *American Journal of Clinical Nutrition* online (March 10, 2010).

236. http://www.praktikos.org.

237. *Harvard Health Letter* (December 2009).

238. http://www.anh-usa.org (October 9, 2012).

239. http://vaers.hhs.gov/index

240. https://www.cbslocal.com (October 4, 2012).

241. http://www.bloomberg.com (September 12, 2012).

242. http://www.nbcnews.com (August 14, 2012).

243. Caroline Baum, Interview, *Bloomberg News* (March 2, 2009).

244. *Forbes* (July 13, 2009): 16.

245. http://www.againstcronycapitalism.org (September 2, 2011).

246. *Economist* (May 9, 2009): 14.

247. *Washington Times* (June 22, 2009): 6-7.

248. Ann Woolner, *Bloomberg News* (May 6, 2009).

249. Lawrence Kudlow, *Washington Times* (May 4, 2009): 31.

250. http://www.bloomberg.com (September 17, 2010).

251. http://www.jalopnik.com (December 3, 2010).

252. *Weekly Standard* (July 13, 2009): 17.

253. http://www.thefiscaltimes.com (October 17, 2012).

254. Sharon Terlep, *Wall Street Journal* as reported in http://www.thefiscaltimes.com (October 17, 2012).

255. http://www.printthis.clickability.com (September 23, 2010).

256. Schweizer, http://www.washingtontimes.com (November 2, 2012).

257. http://www.realclearpolitics.com (May 13, 2010).

258. http://www.washingtonpost.com (November 12, 2010).

259. Ibid.

260. Ibid.

261. http://www.openmarket.org (August 23, 2010).

262. http://www.freebeacon.com (October 8, 2012).

263. Louis Woodhill, http://www.forbes.com (August 15, 2012).

264. http://www.news.yahoo.com (November 13, 2010).

265. http://www.washingtontimes.com (November 26, 2010).

266. *Washington Times* (September 10, 2012): 36.

267. http://www.washingtonexaminer.com (October 25, 2012).

268. *Reuters* (November 7, 2012).

269. Slack, http://www.politico.com (November 6, 2012).

270. Smith, http://www.tricities.com (December 11, 2012); Antoniades, http://www.news.yahoo.com (January 3, 2013).

271. http:/www.wsj.com (August 19, 2012).

272. Labor Union Report, http://www.redstate.com (December 4, 2012).

273. *Weekly Standard* (October 12, 2009): 20.

274. http://www.thedailybeast.com (February 26, 2011).

275. http://www.prospect.org (September 30, 2002).

276. Ibid., 22.

277. Ibid., 24.

278. Moreno, http://www.onlinewsj.com (September 11, 2012).

279. http://www.wsj.com (November 26, 2011).

280. *Weekly Standard* (October 12, 2009) p. 23.

281. Moreno, http://www.onlinewsj.com (September 11, 2012).

282. Ibid., 22.

283. http://www.freebeacon.com (October 18, 2012).

284. Shepardson, http://www.detroitnews.com (January 23, 2013).

285. This and prior estimates published by Senator Jim DeMint (R-South Carolina).

286. Timpf, *Washington Times* (December 17, 2012): 3.

287. http://www.thedailybeast.com (February 26, 2011).

288. Ibid.

289. Staff, http://www.freebeacon.com (November 2, 2012).

290. http://www.wjs.com (April 1, 2011).

291. http://www.vanderstoep.com.

292. *New York Daily News* (September 6, 2011).

293. http://www.chicagotribune.com (September 1, 2011).

294. Ibid., (September 21, 2011).

295. Klopott, et al, http://www.bloomberg.com (December 12, 2012).

296. http://www.bloomberg.com (October 26, 2011).

297. *Weekly Standard* (October 12, 2009): 24.

298. http://www.orangepunch.ocregister.com (May 10, 2011).

299. *Washington Times* (March 15, 2010): 29.

300. Ibid., (June 13, 2011): 38.

301. Ibid.

302. *Weekly Standard* (October 12, 2009): 24.

303. Ibid., 22.

304. *New York Times* (July 1, 2010): A-23.

305. *Weekly Standard* (December 28, 2009): 10.

306. Ibid., (October 12, 2009): 24.

307. George Will, http://www.washingtonpost.com (November 21, 2012).

308. http://www.nationalreview.com (September 10, 2012).

309. *Washington Times* (June 14, 2010): 30.

310. Ibid., 34.

311. Ibid.

312. Ibid., (December 26, 2011): 35.

313. Ibid.; (February 8, 2010): 34.

314. Zekman, http://www.chicago.cbslocal.com (October 29, 2012).

315. http://www.myfox8.com (February 14, 2012).

316. http://blogs.the-american-interest.com (October 25, 2012).

317. Ibid.

318. *Forbes* (May 23, 2011): 101.

319. Shlaes, http://www.bloomberg.com (December 25, 2012).

320. Staff, http://www.freebeacon.com (December 7, 2012).

321. Mead, http://blogs.the-american-interest.com (December 5, 2012).

322. http://www.capitalresearch.org (December 2, 2011); http://www.wsj.com (November 27, 2011).

323. George Will, http://www.washingtonpost.com (December 14, 2012).

324. http://www.baltimore.sun.com (March 5, 2010).

325. http://www.nationalreview.com (October 29, 2012).

326. McMorris, http://www.freebeacon.com (December 17, 2012).

327. *Washington Times* (February 6, 2012): 14.

328. Liebau, http://www.townhall.com (December 7, 2012).

329. http://blogs.wsj.com (June 9, 2010).

330. *Forbes* (June 28, 2010): 21 and Lawrence Kudlow, *Washington Times* (January 23, 2012): 33.

331. *Weekly Standard* (December 21, 2009): 3.

332. *Washington Times*, editorial, (December 21, 2009):38.

333. Richards, http://www.watchdog.org (November 24, 2012).

334. *Washington Times* (March 15, 2010): 3.

335. http://wtop.com on Drudge Report (November 2, 2010).

336. http://www.freebeacon.com (October 18, 2012).

337. *Washington Times* (April 23, 2012): 34.

338. http://www.washingtonpost.com (May 12, 2011).

339. Newby, http://www.examiner.com (November 15, 2012).

340. http://www.jsonline.com (May 11, 2011).

341. http://www.dailycaller.com (January 6, 2012).

342. Hassett, http://www.bloomberg.com (October 11, 2010).

343. http://www.againstcronycapitalism.org (April 13, 2012).

344. Kotkin, http://www.politico.com (September 24, 2010).

345. http://www.politics.usnews.com (September 10, 2010).

346. *Washington Times* (August 22, 2011): 8.

347. http://www.rlc.org/Texas (November 2, 2012); also http://www.wsj.com (November 2, 2012).

348. http://www.againstcronycapitalism.org (October 31, 2012).

349. Ratcliffe, http://www.statesman.com (November 2, 2012).

350. http://www.anh-usa.org (May 15, 2012); also (October 16, 2012).

351. Mulshine, http://blog.nj.com (April 1, 2012).

352. Rugy, http://www/bloomberg.com (December 23, 2010).

353. George Will, http://www.washingtonpost.com (March 28, 2012).

354. http://www.techcrunch.com (October 5, 2012); also http://www.washingtontimes.com (October 5, 2012).

355. Ibid.

356. http://www.washingtonexaminer.com; http://print-this.clickabiliyt.com (August 22, 2010).

357. Bowman, http://www/naplesnews.com (July 23, 2011); data from http://www.opensecrets.org.

358. Copland, Asbestos, http://www.triallawyersinc.com (2008).

359. http://www.triallawyersinc.com (October 2009): No. 8.

360. Copland, Asbestos, http://www.triallawyersinc.com (2005).

361. Ibid., (October 2009): No. 8.

362. Ibid.

363. Ibid.; Junk Science Propelled Edward's Career? http://www.wnd.com (July 7, 2004).

364. Copland, Asbestos, http://www.triallawyersinc.com (2008).

365. http://www.news.yahoo.com (May 9, 2011).

366. Levy, http://www.cato.org (March 6, 1999).

367. Ibid.

368. Ibid.

369. *Forbes* (March 15, 2012): 66.

370. http://www.bitter.queen.typepad.com/friends-of-ours/rule-11/.

371. Ibid.

372. http://www.anh-usa.org (December 2, 2008); and http://www.capoliticalnews.com (April 15, 2012).

373. *Forbes* (May 24, 2010): 70-77.

374. Sidak, *Washington Times* (November 19, 2012): 28.

375. Copland, Report on Litigation Lobby, http://www.triallawyersinc.com (2010); also see Center for Responsive Politics, http://www.opensecrets.org; and National Institute on Money in State Politics, http://www.followthemoney.org.

376. *Washington Examiner* (October 25, 2011); also http://www.manhattan-institute.org.

377. http://www.againstcronycapitalism.org (November 16, 2011).

378. Copland, http://www.wsj.com (February 9, 2010); also http://www.manhattan-institute.org.

379. *Washington Times* (December 20, 2010): 14, citing Center for Responsive Politics.

380. Health Hazard, http://www.triallawyersinc.com (October 2009): No. 8.

381. John Edwards, http://washingtonmonthly.com (October 2001).

382. http://www.triallawyersinc.com (2009 and 2010).

383. The Problem, http://www.commongood.com.

384. Heilprin, http://www.news.yahoo.com (August 21, 2010).

385. *New Scientist* (July 30, 2011): 5; also Sedgwick, http://www.lawsdma.com (May 2, 2011).

386. http://www.abcnews.go.com (October 7, 2010).

387. Hassett, http://www.bloomberg.com (October 25, 2010).

388. Ryley, http://www.thedaily.com (September 10, 2012); also *New York Times* (December 19, 2011): A-1.

389. America the Vulnerable, Government Accountability Institute, (September 5, 2012).

390. Ibid.

391. http://www.thedailybeast.com (October 8, 2012).

392. Aaron Klein, http://www.wnd.com (October 29, 2012).

393. *Washington Times* (April 11, 2011): 32.

394. Runningen, White House press conference, http://www.businessweek.com (September 12, 2011).

395. Billet, http://www.commentarymagazine.com/article/the-war-on-philanthropy/ (July 2009): p. 2.

396. Ibid., 4.

397. Ibid., 3.

398. Yudelson, http://www.jstandard.com (November 14, 2012).

399. Billet, http://commentarymagazine.com/article/the-war-on-philanthropy (July 2009): 2.

400. Goodman, http://healthblog.ncpa.org (July 9, 2012).

401. Guiding Principles, http://www.independentsector.org.

402. http://www.washingtonpost.com (September 6, 2012).

403. Orszag, http://www.bloomberg.com (November 27, 2012).

404. Lane, http://washingtonpost.com (July 30, 2012).

405. *Washington Times* (September 17, 2012): 12.

406. http://www.washingtonguardian.com (August 30, 2012).

407. Streiff, http://www.redstate.com (December 14, 2012).

408. Ibid.

409. *Washington Times* (September 17, 2012): 34.

410. Giammarise, http://www.toledoblade.com (November 12, 2012).

411. Faber, http://www.lewrockwell.com (November 3, 2012).

412. See earlier chapters and Hunter Lewis, *Where Keynes Went Wrong: And Why World Governments Keep Creating Inflation, Bubbles, and Busts* (Mt. Jackson, VA: Axios Press, 2009).

413. Heyes, http://www.naturalnews.com (November 22, 2012).

414. *Washington Times* (July 2, 2012).

415. Staff, http://www.nation.foxnews.com (January 2, 2013).

416. Ibid., (November 7, 2011): 35.

417. http://www.daytondailynews.com (August 27, 2012); also http://www.washingtonexaminer.com (September 27, 2012).

418. Obamaphones, http://www.freebeacon.com (October 8, 2012).

419. *Washington Times* (February 11, 2013): 11.

420. http://www.money.ccn.com (April 12, 2012).

421. Halper, http://weeklystandard.com (October 26, 2012), based on Senate Budget Committee data.

422. Rector, http://www.nypost.com (November 26, 2012).

423. Sowell, http://www/townhall.com (December 12, 2012).

424. Cato Tax and Budget Bulletin (May 2002): No. 7.

425. Bass, http://www.bloomberg.com (October 2, 2012).

426. *New York Times* (July 5, 2010): A-1.

427. David Stockman interview (February 15, 2013).

428. Faber, http://www.bloomberg.com (October 28, 2011); also Ron Paul, http://www.lewrockwell.com (October 10, 2012).

429. *National Journal* (April 28, 2011).

430. George Will, http://www.washingtonpost.com (October 26, 2012); also Boaz, http://cato-at-liberty.org (February 13, 2012); John Goodman, http://healhblog.ncpa.org (September 12, 2012).

431. Study by Lawrence Kotlikoff of Boston University, see http://www.bloomberg.com (August 8, 2012).

432. http://www.concordcoalition.org (2012).

433. Kinsley, http://www/bloomberg.com (January 20, 2012).

434. Ibid.

435. http://www.againstcronycapitalism.org (January 9, 2012); also George Will, http://www.washingtonpost. com (January 6, 2012).

436. Goodman, http://healthblog.ncpa.org (July 6, 2011).

437. Ibid. (July 16, 2012).

438. http://www.money.cnn.com (September 7, 2012).

439. http://www.businessinsider.com (July 6, 2012).

440. http://www.politico.com (November 7, 2012).

441. http://www.againstcronycapatilism.org (May 18, 2012).

442. Bigelow, http://www.townhall.com (November 23, 2012).

443. Ibid.

444. Ibid.

445. *Washington Times* (June 20, 2011): 38.

446. Golden, http://www.bloomberg.com (March 4, 2010).

447. Hechinger, http://www.bloomberg.com (March 26, 2012).

448. Raum, http://www.news.yahoo.com (April 3, 2012).

449. http://www.dailyfinance.com (May 1, 2012).

450. Tom Friedman, Op Ed, *New York Times* (September 9, 2009).

451. http://www.newsobserver.com (September 27, 2011).

452. http://www.newsweek.com (February 26, 2010).

453. http://againstcronycapitalism.org (September 28, 2012).

454. Ibid.

455. Orszag, http://www.tnr.com (September 14, 2011).

456. Will, http://www.washingtonpost.com (June 9, 2011).

457. Robert Skidelsky, *John Maynard Keynes*, vol. 2, *The Economist as Savior 1920–1937* (London: Macmillan, 2000), 224.

458. Bailey, http://blogchristianitytoday.com (April 13, 2008).

459. Ibid.

460. O'Rourke interview, http://www.newyorkpost.com (October 3, 2010).

461. Peter Berkowitz, http://www.realclearpolitics.com (December 10, 2010).

462. Ibid.

463. Will, http://www.washingtonpost.com (March 11, 2010).

464. Quoted in Will Durant, *The Story of Philosophy*, (New York: Simon and Schuster): 655.

465. Scott Rasmussen, respected political polling expert and author, http://www.newsmax.com (September 21, 2012).

466. http://www.john-goodman-blog.com (September 8, 2010).

467. Murray, http://www.washingtonpost.com (October 22, 2010).

468. Codevilla, http://www.spectator.org (August 4, 2010).

469. Marc Farber, *Gloom, Boom, and Doom Report* (May 4, 2011): 10.

470. Jerry Bowyer, http://www.blogs.forbes.com (January 26, 2011).

471. Paul Johnson, *Intellectuals* (New York: Harper and Row, 1988).

472. Ludwig von Mises, *Human Action* (New Haven: Yale University Press, 1963), 193.

473. Hunter Lewis, *Free Prices Now!: Fixing the Economy by Abolishing the Fed* (Edinburg, VA: AC2 Books, 2013).

474. *Business Week* (May 20, 1985): 38.

475. Lester Brown press release, November 6, 2001.

476. John Hobson, *Richard Cobden: The International Man* (London: 1919), 392.

477. *Grant's Interest Rate Observer* (July 13, 2012): 1.

478. Pipes, http://www.forbes.com (August 20, 2012).

479. Smith, http://www.nypost.com (October 2, 2010).

480. See end of John Maynard Keynes's *General Theory of Employment, Interest, and Money* (Amherst, NY: Prometheus Books, 1997).

Index

FDIC (Federal Deposit
Insurance Corpora-
tion) 90, 106
febrile seizures 189
Federal Aviation Adminis-
tration 26
Federal Communications
Commission (FCC)
Lyndon Johnson and
64–66
stimulus money 47–48
Tracfone and 287–288
federal disability program
282–283
Federal Election Commis-
sion 42
Federal Emergency Man-
agement Agency
(FEMA) 78, 235
Federal Express Company
(FedEx) 26, 327
Federal Home Loan Banks
36
Federal Housing Adminis-
tration (FHA) 36, 38
financial condition of
39–40, 43
*Federal Reserve: An Inten-
tional Mystery, The*
326–327
Federal Reserve, US 18,
63, 90, 100, 106, 222,
308, 337–338

deficit financing by
326–327
Fed Funds Rate 36
interest rates and 35–36,
199, 329
money printing by (new
money) 11, 16–17, 319
New York 19, 86, 88,
89, 92
Federal Trade Commis-
sion (FTC) 252
censoring by 334
dairies and 115
Fed Funds Rate 36
Fen-Phen 245
fertility problems 117
Filipino veterans 46, 330
Financial Services Com-
mittee, House 38
finasteride 175
Fink, Larry 29
Finland 48
First Solar 53
Fiscal Cliff 57, 59–62
Fisher, Linda J. 114
Fisker 48
flame retardants 121, 328
Florida 129, 247, 285, 297
flu
deaths 186–187
H1N1 virus and 188

M